BALLOON FLYING HANDBOOK

2001

U.S. DEPARTMENT OF TRANSPORTATION
FEDERAL AVIATION ADMINISTRATION
Flight Standards Service

For sale by the Superintendent of Documents, U.S. Government Printing Office
Internet: bookstore.gpo.gov Phone: (202) 512-1800 Fax: (202) 512-2250
Mail: Stop SSOP, Washington, DC 20402-0001

ISBN 0-16-050838-X

PREFACE

This Balloon Flying Handbook introduces the basic pilot knowledge and skills that are essential for piloting balloons. It introduces pilots to the broad spectrum of knowledge that will be needed as they progress in their pilot training. This handbook is for student pilots, as well as those pursuing more advanced pilot certificates.

Student pilots learning to fly balloons, certificated pilots preparing for additional balloon ratings or who desire to improve their flying proficiency and aeronautical knowledge, and commercial balloon pilots teaching balloon students how to fly should find this handbook helpful. This book introduces the prospective pilot to the realm of balloon flight and provides information and guidance to all balloon pilots in the performance of various balloon maneuvers and procedures.

This handbook conforms to pilot training and certification concepts established by the Federal Aviation Administration (FAA). There are different ways of teaching, as well as performing flight procedures and maneuvers, and many variations in the explanations of aerodynamic theories and principles. This handbook adopts a selective method and concept to flying balloons. The discussions and explanations reflect the most commonly used practices and principles. Occasionally, the word *must* or similar language is used where the desired action is deemed critical. The use of such language is not intended to add to, interpret, or relieve a duty imposed by Title 14 of the Code of Federal Regulations (14 CFR).

It is essential for persons using this handbook to also become familiar with and apply the pertinent parts of 14 CFR and the Aeronautical Information Manual (AIM). Performance standards for demonstrating competence required for pilot certification are prescribed in the appropriate balloon practical test standard.

The FAA gratefully acknowledges Brent Stockwell, Christine Kalakuka, and the Balloon Publishing Company for giving permission to use parts of their book entitled "How to Fly a Balloon."

The current Flight Standards Service airman training and testing material, and subject matter knowledge codes for all airman certificates and ratings can be obtained from the Regulatory Support Division, AFS-600, home page on the Internet.

The Regulatory Support Division's Internet address is: http://afs600.faa.gov

Comments regarding this handbook should be sent to U.S. Department of Transportation, Federal Aviation Administration, Airman Testing Standards Branch, AFS-630, P.O. Box 25082, Oklahoma City, OK 73125.

This handbook can be purchased from the Superintendent of Documents, U.S. Government Printing Office (GPO), Washington, DC 20402-9325, or from U.S. Government Bookstores located in major cities throughout the United States.

AC 00-2, Advisory Circular Checklist, transmits the current status of FAA advisory circulars and other flight information and publications. This checklist is free of charge and may be obtained by sending a request to U.S. Department of Transportation, Subsequent Distribution Office, SVC-121.23, Ardmore East Business Center, 3341 Q 75th Avenue, Landover, MD 20785. The checklist is also available on the Internet at http://www.faa.gov/abc/ac-chklst/actoc.htm

CONTENTS

CHAPTER 5—POSTFLIGHT PROCEDURES

CHAPTER 6—SPECIAL OPERATIONS

CHAPTER 7—REGULATIONS AND MAINTENANCE

CHAPTER 8—EARNING A PILOT CERTIFICATE

CHAPTER 9—AERONAUTICAL DECISION MAKING

APPENDIX A

APPENDIX B

APPENDIX C

APPENDIX D

CHAPTER 1

INTRODUCTION TO BALLOONING

This chapter presents an introduction to ballooning's history, physics, basic balloon terms, balloon components, support equipment, and choosing a balloon.

HISTORY

The first manned aircraft was a hot air balloon. This balloon was built by the Montgolfier Brothers and flown by Pilatre de Rozier and the Marquis d'Arlandes on November 21, 1783, in France, over 120 years before the Wright Brothers' first flight. The balloon envelope was paper, and the fuel was straw which was burned in the middle of a large circular basket. Only 10 days later, Professor Jacques Charles launched the first gas balloon made of a varnished silk envelope filled with hydrogen. Thus, the two kinds of balloons flown today—hot air and gas—were developed in the same year.

Gas ballooning became a sport for the affluent and flourished on a small scale in Europe and the United States. Gas balloons were used by the military in the Siege of Paris, the U.S. Civil War, and World Wars I and II. In the last few decades, gas ballooning has been practiced primarily in Europe, particularly in the town of Augsburg, Germany, where an active club has arranged with a local factory to purchase hydrogen gas at a low price.

At the turn of the century, the *smoke balloon*—a canvas envelope heated by a fire on the ground—was a common county fair opening event. Today, there are only a few people who have ridden on the trapeze of a smoke balloon (called a hot air balloon without airborne heater). After the initial climb—about 3,000 feet per minute (FPM)—the hot air cools and the rider separates from the balloon, deploying a parachute to return to earth. Two chase crews were standard, one for the performer and one for the envelope.

In the 1950s, the U.S. Navy contracted with the General Mills Company to develop a small hot air balloon for military purposes. The Navy never used the balloon, but the project created the basis for the modern hot air balloon.

With the use of modern materials and technology, hot air ballooning has become an increasingly popular sport.

PHYSICS

Essentially there are two kinds of balloons: hot air balloons and gas balloons. There is also the smoke balloon, which is a hot air balloon without an airborne heater, and the solar balloon, but they are rare and almost nonexistent. This handbook primarily covers hot air balloons.

Gas is defined as a substance possessing perfect molecular mobility and the property of indefinite expansion, as opposed to a solid or liquid.

The most popular gas used in ballooning is hot air. As the air is heated, it expands making it less dense. Because it has fewer molecules per given volume, it weighs less than non-heated ambient air (air that surrounds an object) and is lighter in weight.

As the air inside a balloon envelope is heated, it becomes lighter than the outside air the envelope, causing the balloon to rise. The greater the heat differential between the air inside the envelope and the air outside, the faster the balloon rises.

Hot air is constantly being lost from the top of the envelope by leaking through the fabric, seams, and deflation port. Heat is also being lost by radiation. Only the best and newest fabrics are nearly airtight. Some fabrics become increasingly porous with age and some colors radiate heat faster than others do. Under certain conditions, some dark-colored envelopes may gain heat from the sun. To compensate for heat loss, prolonged flight is possible only if fuel is carried on board to make heat.

To change altitude, the internal temperature of the air in the envelope is raised to climb, or allowed to cool to descend. Cooling of the envelope is also possible by allowing hot air to escape through a vent. This temporary opening closes and seals automatically when it is not in use.

BASIC BALLOON TERMS

Balloon terms vary because proprietary terms and foreign terms have entered the language of ballooning. However, consistency in terminology is important because it makes it easier for the pilot, crew, and passengers to communicate with each other. The most common terms are used in the text and in the generic illustrations (refer to figure 1-1) in this handbook. Terms and names used by manufacturers are also included. The glossary contains balloon and aeronautical terms.

BALLOON COMPONENTS

A hot air balloon consists of three main components: envelope, heater system, and basket.

Envelope

The envelope is the fabric portion of the balloon containing the hot air and is usually made of nylon. The deflation port is located at the top of the envelope and allows for the controlled release of hot air. It is covered by the deflation panel sometimes called a top cap, parachute top, or spring top (refer to figures 1-2, 1-3, and 1-4). In a balloon with a parachute top, partial opening of the parachute valve is the normal way to cool the balloon. Balloons with other types of deflation panels may have a cooling vent in the side or the top.

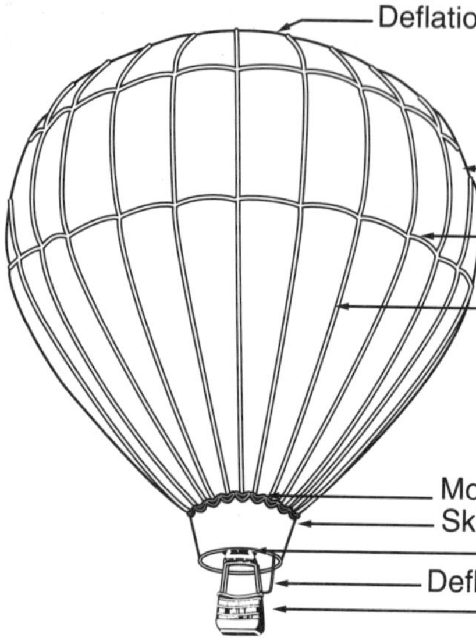

FIGURE 1-1.—Basic Balloon Terms.

Heater System

The heater system consists of one or more burners that burn propane, fuel tanks that store liquid propane, and fuel lines that carry the propane from the tanks to the burners. The burners convert cold (or ambient) air into hot air, which in turn provides the lift required for flight.

Basket

The basket (usually made of wickerwork rattan) contains the fuel tanks, instruments, pilot, and passengers.

SUPPORT EQUIPMENT

Standard support equipment for ballooning is a an inflation fan, transport/chase vehicle, and small miscellaneous items, such as igniters, drop lines, gloves, spare parts, and helmets.

Inflation Fan

Fans come in different styles and sizes. Your finances, style of inflation, and size of the balloon will determine the best fan for you.

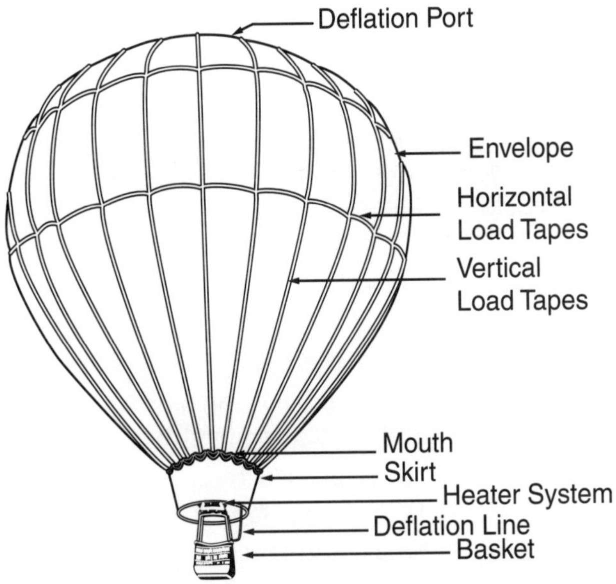

FIGURE 1-2.—Rip Panel Envelope Design.

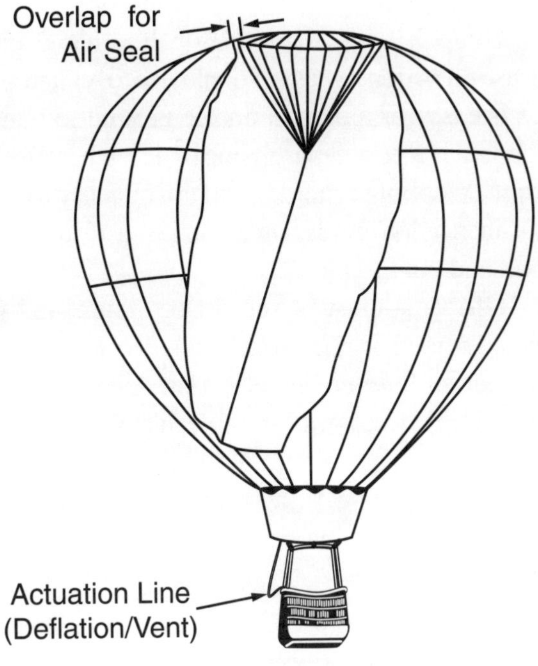

FIGURE 1-3.—Parachute Top Envelope Design.

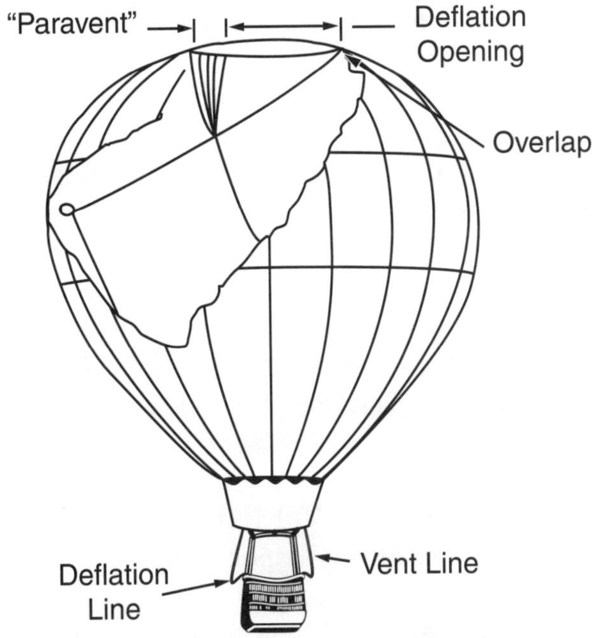

FIGURE 1-4.—Spring Top Envelope Design.

Points to consider in selecting a fan are:

- **Weight**—Someone will have to lift the fan into and out of the transport vehicle. Wheels do not help with the weight and are not helpful on soft ground. One person can carry a small fan, but a larger fan may take two people.
- **Safety**—Fan blades today can be wood, aluminum, fiberglass, or composite, with wood being the most popular. Wood or aluminum blades designed specifically for balloon fan use are best. The fan should have a cowling of fiberglass or metal. A cage or grill alone is not sufficient to contain rocks or pieces of blade.
- **Transport**—Space available in a pickup truck, the back of a van, or on a trailer may determine the size of the fan.
- **Cubic Feet Per Minute (CFM)**—Fan blade design, duct design, and engine speed determine the amount of air moved in a given time. Do not confuse engine size with CFM. Larger engines do not necessarily push more air. Moving a high volume of air is not necessarily the ultimate goal in fan performance. Some people prefer a slower cold inflation to allow for a thorough preflight inspection.

- **Fan Maintenance**—The inflation fan is the most dangerous piece of equipment in ballooning. A good fan requires little maintenance and should be easy to maintain. Check the oil periodically and change it once a year. Check hub bolts and grill screws for tightness on a regular basis.
- **Fuel**—Gasoline smells, spills, pollutes, and degrades in storage. Do not store gasoline in the fan due to fire hazard and the formation of varnish, which can clog fuel passages. Some gasoline fans can be converted to propane. Propane is clean, stores in a sealed tank, and does not change with age.

Transport/Chase Vehicle

Balloon ground transportation varies. The most common vehicles are a van with the balloon carried inside, a pickup truck with the balloon carried in the bed, or a van or pickup truck with a small trailer (flatbed or covered).

Some considerations in selecting a transport/chase vehicle are:

- **Finances**—If you are on a tight budget, a trailer hitch on the family sedan and a small flatbed trailer may work just fine.
- **Convenience**—For ease of handling the balloon, a small flatbed trailer that is low to the ground makes the least lifting demands on you and your crew.
- **Number of Crew Members**—If the number of crew members is small, handling the balloon should be made as easy as possible. If the number of crew members is large, the size of the chase vehicle and other factors may be more important.
- **Storage**—Some balloonists, who do not have room for inside storage, and want security on the road, choose an enclosed trailer. If you choose an enclosed trailer for the storage of your balloon, the trailer should be a light color to help reduce the heat inside.
- **Fuel**—A propane-powered vehicle gives the option of fueling the balloon from the vehicle.
- **Vehicle Suitability**—Terrain, vehicle road clearance, and number of chase crew members are factors that will determine the suitability of a transport/ chase vehicle.

Miscellaneous Items

- **Igniters**—It is recommended that you carry at least two sources of ignition on board. The best igniter is the plain and simple welding striker. Many new balloons have built-in piezo ignition systems.
- **Fueling Adapter**—Pilots should carry their own adapters to ensure that the adapters are clean and not worn. Adapters that are dirty and worn may damage a fuel system.
- **Fire Extinguisher**—Some balloons come with a small fire extinguisher affixed in the basket. However, they are usually too small to extinguish grass fires or serious basket fires caused by a propane leak. Fumbling for a fire extinguisher may just use up the time required to manually extinguish a propane-leak fire before it becomes serious. Most propane fires can be extinguished by turning off a valve.
- **First Aid Kit**—Some pilots carry a small first aid kit in their balloon, some in the chase vehicle. This is a matter of personal preference. A kit's contents are often a topic at safety seminars and may vary from region to region.
- **Drop Line**—A good drop line has a quick release provision, is easy to deploy, recover and store, and is easy for a person on the ground to handle. Webbing is a popular drop line material because it is strong. Webbing is hard to roll up, but easy to store. Half-inch nylon braid is strong and is easily rolled into a ball and put in a bag.
- **Gloves**—Gloves should be made of light-colored smooth leather to reflect/deflect propane, and gauntlet-style to cover the wrist. Avoid synthetic material which melts in heat and ventilated gloves which let in flame or gas.
- **Spares**—The following are recommended spares to carry in the chase vehicle or to have on hand.

    - Quick pins and carabiners.
    - Gloves and helmets.
    - Envelope fabric.
    - Spare tire for the trailer.
    - Extra fuel for the fan.

- **Helmets**—Some balloon manufacturers suggest protective headgear be worn, especially in high-wind conditions. The intention is to protect heads from impact injury. Store helmets in a bag that can be carried inside or outside the basket, depending on number of passengers and available room.

CHOOSING A BALLOON

Many companies manufacture balloons that are type-certificated by the Federal Aviation Administration (FAA). A type-certificated balloon has passed many tests, has been approved by the FAA, and conforms to the manufacturer's Type Certificate Data Sheet (TCDS). Balloon size is rated by envelope volume. Following are the most popular sizes in use today.

Category	No. People	Cubic Ft. (Approximately)
AX5	1	42,372
AX6	1-2	56,496
AX7	3-4	77,682
AX8	5-7	105,30
AX9	7-10	211,860

Advantages of Balloon Sizes

Different balloon sizes offer different advantages. The size of the balloon purchased should be determined according to planned use(s). Most pilots think smaller balloons are easier to handle, fly, and pack-up. Bigger balloons use less fuel, operate cooler, and last longer. If you live in higher elevations or hotter climates, or if you plan to carry passengers, a larger balloon is preferred. If you plan to compete in balloon competitions or fly only for sport, a smaller balloon is more practical.

Selecting a New or Used Balloon

Should you buy a new or used balloon? The cost is the most obvious difference between new and used balloons. Some new pilots buy a used balloon to gain proficiency, and then purchase a new balloon when they have a better idea of what they want or need.

Balloon Brands

The level of after-sales service available—locally and from the manufacturer—is an important criterion in deciding which brand of balloon you should purchase. Talk to local pilots and ask questions. How does the local balloon repair station feel about different brands? Do they stock parts for only one brand? Does the manufacturer ship parts and fabric for balloons already in the field, or do they reserve these parts and fabric for new production? Will your balloon be grounded for lack of materials while new balloons are being built?

There are other criteria that could be considered, such as altitude at which the balloon will be flying, climate, and interchangeability of components, to give some examples. Before making your final decision, talk to people with different kinds of balloons and who do different kinds of flying. Crewing for different balloons is an excellent way to learn about the various kinds of balloons. Crewing on different balloons may help you decide on your first balloon purchase.

CHAPTER 2

PREPARING FOR FLIGHT

This chapter introduces elements the balloon pilot needs to consider when preparing for a flight. The sections include flight planning, preflight operations, the use of a checklist, preflight inspection, the crew, and the chase.

FLIGHT PLANNING

Flight planning starts long in advance of the night before the launch. Title 14 of the Code of Federal Regulations (14 CFR) part 91, section 91.103 states: "Each pilot in command shall, before beginning a flight, become familiar with all available information concerning that flight...." The following paragraphs outline various elements to be considered in flight planning.

Weather

A good balloonist pays constant attention to the weather. You should begin to study the weather several days before the day of the flight. Weather runs in cycles and understanding the cycles in your area will help you make successful flights.

Weather background preparation

- Visit the nearest National Weather Service (NWS) office and FAA Automated Flight Service Station (AFSS).
- Check the library for books about weather in your specific area.
- Talk with pilots of other types of aircraft; talk with farmers, sailors, and fishermen, if appropriate.
- Watch local television weather shows, particularly the 5-day forecasts.
- Listen to local radio weather information.
- Read the weather section of the local newspaper.

Specific weather preparation

- On the evening before a flight call an AFSS for an outlook briefing (6 or more hours before the proposed launch—know what hours an AFSS makes new information available).
- Devote particular attention to television or radio weather reports the night before a flight.
- Locate and use automated weather stations: NWS, Automatic Terminal Information Service (ATIS), Automatic Weather Observing System (AWOS), Harbor Masters, Highway Department, and State Parks.
- On the morning of a flight, phone an AFSS for a Standard Briefing.
- On the way to the launch site, develop weather observation points, such as a tree in someone's yard, smoke at a factory, or a flag at a car dealership.
- At the launch site, check a windsock or tetrahedron, talk with other pilots, or send up a pilot balloon (pibal). Observe smoke, flags, or other balloons.

Weather record keeping

- Compare predictions to actual weather.
- Compare past predictions to future predictions and make your own prediction.
- Compare reports from nearby reporting stations to actual weather at your launch site.

Weather preflight briefing

Before each flight get a complete briefing from weather sources in the local area. See appendix A for sample weather briefing checklists that you can used as a guides to develop your own personal forms for recording weather briefings.

Equipment

Pack all equipment and have it ready the night before a flight. Check to see that the balloon, fan, and vehicle are fueled; vehicle tires are inflated; required documentation is in the balloon; and all necessary maps, radios, and other equipment are loaded in your chase vehicle.

Launch Site

Most balloonists fly regularly from several known launch sites. Unless you launch from a public airport or public balloon area, renew permission to use the site(s) on a regular basis. Do not assume because another pilot uses a certain launch area that anyone can automatically use it.

Purpose of Flight

Preflight planning may vary slightly according to the flight's purpose. If you are carrying passengers, you need to tell them where and when to meet. If you are flying in an organized event, you need to carry your airworthiness and registration certificates with you in case you are required to show them. Also, make sure that your maintenance and insurance records (documentation not normally carried in the balloon) are available for inspection.

Special Circumstances

Most balloon flying is in relatively unhostile terrain and in relatively clement weather. The special circumstances described may be normal for a small percentage of pilots.

Mountain flying

You should plan for the possibility of not being met by the chase crew at the landing site, since following a balloon can be difficult in mountainous terrain. Most pilots carry some additional equipment in the balloon that they do not carry on flatland flights. Suggested provisions and equipment are water, some additional warm clothing or a sleeping bag, a strobe, a radio, a compass, a lightweight shelter (a mylar sheet can be made into a simple tent, for example), and a good map or maps of the area. Pilot and crew should agree on a lost balloon plan.

Cold weather flying

The two main considerations for cold weather flying are keeping the pilot, crew, and passengers warm, and maintaining adequate pressure in the balloon's fuel system.

Layered clothing that entraps warm air is standard cold-weather gear. A hat is important, as significant body heat escapes from the head. Warm gloves and footwear are a must. Remember to have antifreeze in the chase vehicle. Carry chains, a shovel, and a windshield wiper/scraper if there is a possibility of snow.

As propane gets colder, it has less pressure. To ensure adequate pressure in cold weather, add nitrogen (using manufacturer-approved kits), heat the propane, or keep the propane warm. There are several sources that offer tank covers and heating coils. Inspect electrically heated tank covers often, as normal wear and tear and tie-down straps can cause an electrical short circuit, which could start a serious fire during heating. Use tank heaters with extra care. Never heat your tanks within 50 feet of an open flame, or near an appliance with a pilot light, or in a closed room without natural ventilation.

Flying in New Territory

Before making a flight in an area that is new to you, make sure balloonists are welcome. Talk to local balloonists. To locate local balloonists:

- Call the nearest Flight Standards District Office (FSDO)—ask for the name of a balloon pilot examiner or aviation safety counselor.
- Look in the yellow pages under balloons.
- Check for local balloon clubs in the area.

If there are no balloonists in the local area, talk to other pilots or local law enforcement offices. Let them know you are planning a flight and ask their advice.

Clothing

Pilot, crew, and passengers need to dress sensibly. Proper clothing protects participants from burns, poison oak/ivy, and other harmful plants. If it becomes necessary to walk or hike from a landing site inaccessible by the chase vehicle, proper clothing and footwear makes the task easier and less hazardous.

Personal Health

You need to be in good health and well-rested before making a flight. If you do not feel well, do not fly. You will not be at your best and may make mistakes. Get a good night's sleep before making a flight.

PREFLIGHT OPERATIONS

The *preflight*, as an aeronautical term, is generally agreed to be the airworthiness check of an aircraft immediately before flight. In the broadest sense, preflight is everything accomplished in preparation for a flight. In this chapter, preflight operations are operations that occur at the balloon launch site, up to and including the preflight inspection.

Wind Direction

Consider the wind direction before the balloon is even unloaded from the chase vehicle. Take into account the surface wind at the time of cold inflation to avoid carrying a heavy balloon bag and basket around. A *Murphy's Law* type of rule is that the wind will always change during inflation. Local knowledge is invaluable. If other balloons are around, check with the most experienced local pilot.

A wind change at or shortly after sunrise is normal in many places. If you lay your balloon out before sunrise, a wind change may be likely. If you are flying in a new place, watch the local pilots. They may have knowledge that you should heed.

Some general trends are that air usually flows downhill or down valley, first thing in the morning, and air usually flows from cold to warm in the morning. This air drainage may stop very shortly after the sun rises and starts heating the ground. This early morning wind may come from a different direction than the prevailing or predicted wind.

Some local pilots may lay their balloons out in a direction that does not match the airflow at the time, but that will be correct 15 to 30 minutes later when the sunrise change occurs and the inflation starts. Pibals (small balloons filled with helium) are excellent low-level wind direction indicators.

Launch Site

When selecting a launch site factors to consider are obstacles in direction of flight (power lines, buildings, towers, etc.), available landing sites, overhead airspace, and the launch site surface. After considering landing sites and airspace, the launch site surface is the most important.

Launch Site Surface

After determining the wind direction, the next condition that determines the details of the balloon layout is the actual launch site surface. Of course, all pilots wish they could always lay out their balloon on clean, dry, short, green grass. Most pilots are not that fortunate unless they have their own launch site and never fly from different places. Wise pilots modify their techniques to match available conditions, or they have more than one layout procedure to adapt to various launch sites.

Whether flying from a regular launch site, a brand-new location, or from an assigned square at a rally, check the ground for items that may damage or soil the balloon. Look for and remove nails, sharp rocks, twigs, branches, and other foreign objects. If there are patches of oil or other substances, cover them with pieces of carpet, floor mats from the chase vehicle, tarps, or the envelope bag. Some pilots cover the ground where they lay out their balloon with a large tarp every time they fly.

Unless flying at a known site, do not assume it is all right to drive the chase vehicle directly onto the launch area. There are some locations (a soft athletic field, for example) where it is necessary to carry the balloon onto the launch area. In any case, once the balloon and fan are unloaded, drive the chase vehicle out of the launch area so it is not an obstacle to your balloon or other balloons.

Removing the Balloon from the Vehicle

Plan ahead for removing and carrying the balloon from the vehicle to the launch site to avoid unnecessary lifting and moving.

For instance, if you carry the envelope in a bag separate from the basket, drop off the envelope about 15 feet downwind from the basket; this requires less carrying than if it is set down too close to the basket. If the basket and envelope are not connected, the separate pieces are easier to lift and each piece can then be placed in the appropriate position, requiring less moving and carrying.

Assembly

If the balloon is disassembled for transport and handling, it must be assembled in accordance with the flight manual prior to layout. Make sure all fittings and fastenings are secure.

Layout

Do not drag the envelope along the ground when pulling the envelope out of the bag. Many envelopes have holes and tears caused by being dragged over sharp objects while getting the envelope out of the bag. Lift the bag clear of the ground and carry it unless the launch surface is perfect with no sharp objects or dirty spots.

There are many variations to laying out a balloon and preparing it for inflation. The manufacturer of the balloon or the way the balloon is assembled sets some of these inflation styles.

The launch site surface, the order in which the balloon is assembled, and how the balloon is removed from the chase vehicle, has a bearing on the way the preflight layout and inspection proceeds. There is no one best way to lay out a balloon, just as there is no one best way to inflate a balloon. The two most common ways to prepare the balloon for cold inflation are to spread it out, or inflate from a long strip.

Spread layout

The spread layout method for inflation is the most widely used method. By handling the envelope with the load tapes, you can pull the fabric away from the center until the envelope takes its normal shape while still flat on the ground. Exercise care when sliding the fabric across the ground to avoid causing damage.

All balloons have an even number of load tapes. By using the number on the load tape when spreading the envelope, you can arrange to have the envelope in a proper position for inflation. With one crewmember on each side of the envelope's fabric, start at the mouth and travel the length of the appropriate load tape, pulling the fabric taut up to the equator. This gets the bottom laid out flat. Be careful to handle only the load tapes when positioning the envelope because pulling on the fabric could cause damage.

Check the deflation system at this time and properly position it in accordance with the balloon flight manual. While the envelope is filling with air, your crew can assist this process by lifting upward on the load tapes, allowing more cold air to pack the envelope. This method allows the envelope to deploy smoothly and easily, even with a small sized inflation fan.

Strip layout

When inflating on pavement or from a small or narrow launch site, many pilots prefer not to deploy the envelope on the ground. Instead, they prefer to pull the envelope straight out from the basket, making sure the top gore is on top its full length, and to inflate the envelope entirely with the fan. This may require a larger fan, depending on the size of the balloon and envelope material.

Once the balloon is stretched out, make sure that the control lines (deflation, cooling, or rotating) are correctly attached to the basket, according to the manufacturer's instructions. This method minimizes handling the fabric on a rough or dirty surface. It requires more diligence by the ground crew to make sure it deploys correctly.

Progressive fill

Inflate out-of-the-bag is a technique in which the envelope suspension is connected to the basket. The envelope is pulled progressively out of the bag as the fan is running and inflating the envelope as the crew slowly, with pauses, carries the balloon bag away from the basket while the envelope fills.

Another variation of the progressive fill has the crew holding the envelope in their arms, gradually releasing more and more of the envelope, from mouth to top, until the very top of the envelope is released for filling.

Role of the inflator fan

The type of fan needed for different layout techniques depends primarily on the amount of work required by the fan. The strip layout method requires a large, strong fan to force the envelope into shape, while the spread-it-out method requires less fan energy.

CHECKLISTS

The value of using a checklist is well known to the airlines and the military. Regulations require air carrier pilots and military pilots to use checklists. Also, FAA practical tests require pilot certificate applicants to use checklists. Checklists are effective and contribute to safe flying because routine and familiarity breed complacency. Like military and airline pilots, balloonists who fly everyday need a checklist to assure nothing is omitted. For example, professional balloon ride operators are subject to distractions and interruptions during their preflight, layout, assembly, and inspection.

Appendix B contains sample checklists that can be used as is, or adapted to your particular balloon and style.

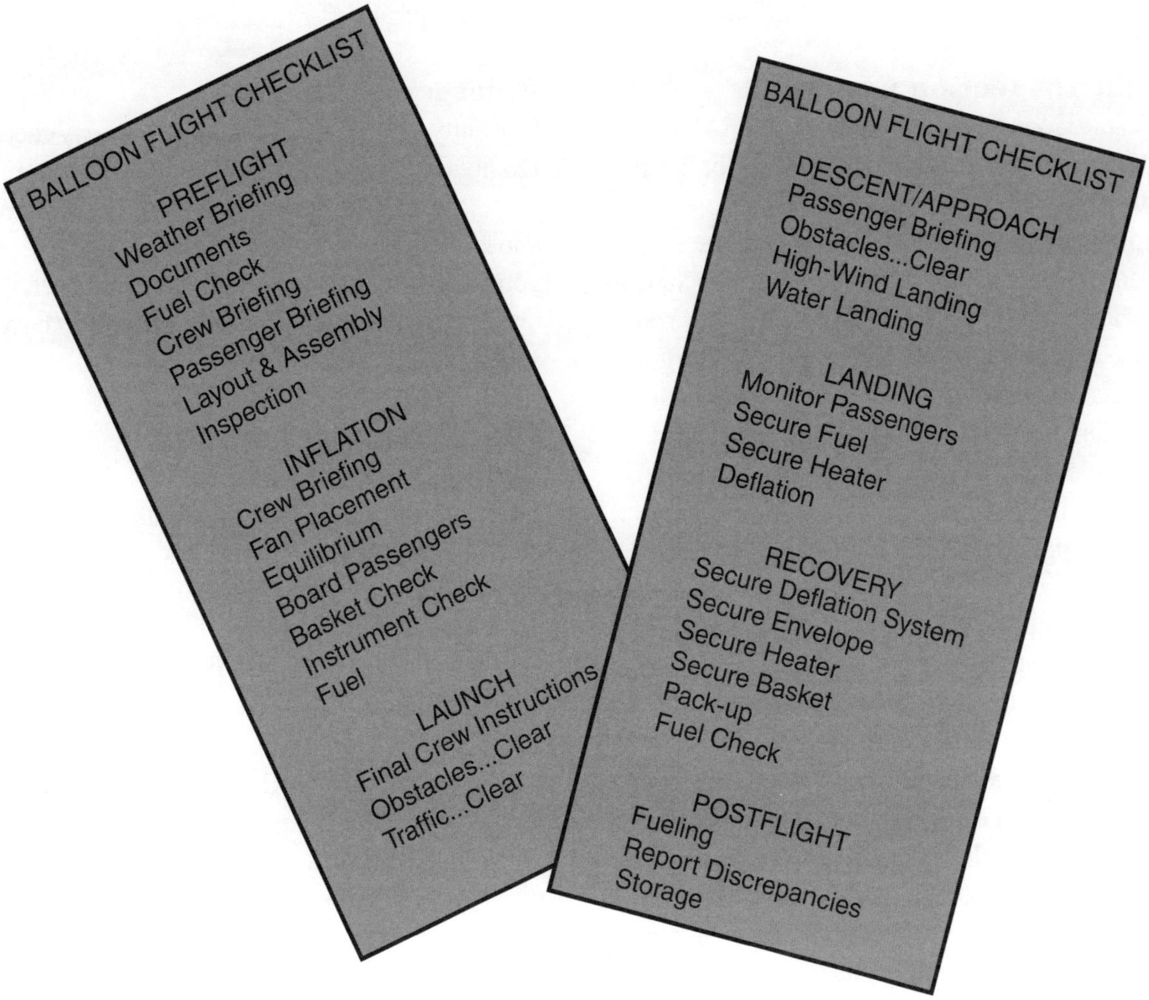

FIGURE 2-1.—Sample Checklists.

Infrequent balloon flyers, which include most balloonists, need checklists because long periods of inactivity creates memory lapses. A typical balloonist may make only 30 to 40 flights per year. A checklist will not replace proficiency, but it will help.

Students and new pilots need checklists because they are forming habit patterns, and need prompting to reinforce training and confirm good habits. [Figure 2-1]

A checklist can save time. By arranging the layout, assembly, and inspection in a logical order, and by accomplishing more than one task at a time, duplication and wasted time can be minimized. For instance, a properly arranged preflight checklist can include many tasks that are performed while the fan is running, so people are not just standing around waiting for the envelope to inflate. Also, a checklist eliminates needless walking. Sometimes pilots circle the envelope three or four times when one lap around should suffice.

Preflight Inspection Checklist

Title 14 of the Code of Federal Regulations (14 CFR) and the practical test standards (PTSs) for balloon pilot certification require the pilot to inspect the balloon by systematically following an appropriate checklist prior to each flight. Most balloon manufacturers include a preflight inspection checklist in the flight manual. You should use this as the basis for your own preflight checklist. Each balloon manufacturer lists maximum allowable damage with which a balloon may fly and still be considered airworthy. Balloon owners should memorize the manufacturer's maximum allowable damage rules and abide by them.

Using a written checklist, the pilot should make certain that the balloon is correctly laid out for inflation, all control lines are attached, the fuel system is operating correctly, maximum allowable damage limits are not exceeded, and there are no nearby obstacles directly downwind. The pilot is responsible for all aspects of flight, including preflight operations. If you are using a new crew, it is necessary to spend more time with them to make sure they understand their duties. Whether using your own experienced crew or a new crew at a rally, it is the pilot's responsibility to ensure the balloon is correctly prepared for inflation and flight.

At this point, you make sure the chase vehicle is clear of the launch site, the keys are in the chase car or with the chase crew, passengers are nearby, and inflation crew is properly dressed and ready. You are now ready to proceed with inflation.

Proper use of a checklist makes the pilot and crew look more professional. If everyone is doing his or her job without excess conversation, confusion, and repetition, the entire scene builds confidence in everyone involved.

The best checklist is the one you write for your balloon, your crew, and your style of flying. A good source for checklist items is the manufacturer of the balloon. Also, you can combine checklists from other pilots and manufacturers into your personal checklist.

Remember that a checklist is a living document that may change or grow when modifications or additions are appropriate.

Emergency Checklist

Carefully study and memorize emergency checklists. Do not try to read a checklist during an emergency; that is for an aircraft with two- or three-person crews and lots of altitude. During an emergency, take prompt action, and when the situation permits, refer to the checklist to ensure that all necessary items have been accomplished.

CREW

Almost all balloon flights are accomplished with a crew. There are a few rugged individuals who inflate their balloon alone, make a flight, pack-up the balloon, and hitchhike back to the launch site, but they are rare. The crew is an essential part of ballooning. They should be well-trained and treated with respect and understanding.

Generally, there are two different areas of responsibility for a crew: inflation/launch and chase/recovery. Both are usually referred to as ground crew. Passengers often serve as inflation crew, become passengers for the flight, and crew again after the balloon has landed.

Number of Crewmembers

The crew consists of people who help with the inflation, chase, and recovery. Some pilots appoint a *crew chief*, normally the most experienced crewmember, but this is a matter of preference. A crew chief is responsible for other crewmembers, organizing the chase, and supervising the recovery. Remember though, the responsibility for all aspects of the flight, including ground operations, rests with you, the pilot.

The number of crewmembers is a matter of individual preference and depends upon the size of the balloon, purpose of the flight, terrain, and other factors. When using a small balloon for instruction, a crew of three people, including the instructor, student, and one crew, is sufficient. For passenger flights in large balloons, a larger number of crewmembers is generally required. Some experienced chase crews prefer to chase alone, some prefer someone along to read a map. Having too many people in the chase vehicle can be a distraction for the driver, who is concentrating on staying near the balloon.

Clothing

Crewmembers should be clothed for safety and comfort. Cover or restrain long hair. Wear only long sleeves and long trousers made of cotton and not synthetic material. Try to wear clothes in layers since temperatures can change quite a bit from before sunrise to during the recovery. Proper clothing protects participants from burns, poison oak/ivy, and other harmful plants.

All crewmembers should wear gloves, preferably smooth leather, loose fitting, and easy to remove. Wear comfortable and protective footwear. If it becomes necessary to walk or hike from a landing site inaccessible by the chase vehicle, proper clothing and footwear makes the task easier and less hazardous.

Crew Briefings

Crew briefings vary from a few last minute instructions (to an experienced, regular crew), or a long, detailed discourse on how to layout, assemble, inflate, chase, recover, and pack a balloon. You can give crew briefings by telephone the night before, or in the chase vehicle on the way to the launch site, but most crew briefings are done at the launch site prior to the flight. It is important for the pilot to remember who is ultimately responsible for the entire operation and that the crew is the pilot's representative on the ground.

Written instructions are a good way to help the crew while the pilot is aloft. Keep a loose-leaf, three-ring binder in the chase vehicle containing crew instructions and maps. This is a useful aid to an inexperienced crewmember. A sample balloon ground crew information sheet is provided. [Figure 2-2]

Types of Flight

The type of flight is important to the crew, so they know the goals of the operation; the possible time aloft; the probable direction(s) of flight; probable altitudes; communications, if any, to be used; and useful maps or charts.

Balloon flights can be classified into several different types: paid passenger, instruction, race, rally, advertising/promotion, and fun.

Many balloon pilots defray the cost of the sport by offering paid passenger rides. The crew should know that these passengers are paying for the privilege, and may have been promised a certain type and length of flight.

Instructional flights require that the crew follow the direction of the instructor, so the student may see and participate as much as possible. The crew should work closely with the instructor and student and not take over any portion of the operation, thus denying the student the opportunity to learn.

For races, crew responsibilities may be different. The pilot may have only a single goal in mind and will zero-in on that goal. The crew's job is always to help the pilot, but in the case of the race flight, the crew should try to relieve the pilot of some of the routine tasks so he or she may concentrate on the competition.

Many rallies, require pilots to carry passengers. Sometimes passengers can be part of the inflation crew. In any case you and your crew should treat them graciously as they are, one way or another, paying

BALLOON GROUND CREW INFORMATION SHEET

ELEMENTS OF CREWING

Timeliness

The crew should arrive on time. The pilot should not have to start out the morning with the stress of a late crew.

Dress

The crew should dress sensibly with long trousers and long sleeve clothing made of natural (non-synthetic) fibers, sturdy boots or shoes, and gloves. Before the burner is used, long sleeves should be down, gloves on, and hair protected.

Public Relations Skills

The crew should smile, wave to farmers, people on tractors, law enforcement, anyone else who is watching the balloon, and be polite at all times. The regular crew should know about the balloon, the pilot, pertinent laws and regulations, be able to correctly answer questions, and be a good representative for ballooning.

Media

The crew should be polite when dealing with the media, and refer questions to the pilot. Anything said to the media may become public record. There is no such thing as *off the record.*

Postflight Responsibility

The crew should remember that there is a balloon to pack-up and a vehicle to drive. The landing site should be cleared and vacated as soon as possible. Make sure you do not leave a mess.

SPECIFIC PROCEDURES

Inflation and Launch

- Keep your back to the flame.
- Never wrap a rope or line around your wrist or any part of your body.
- Keep feet off the balloon and clear of cables and lines.
- Keep chase vehicle clear of launch site and flightpath.
- Do not stand in front of a moving balloon.
- Never turn your back to a balloon that is launching.
- Do not drive on runways or taxiways at airports.

Chase

- Drive first; watch the balloon second.
- Park off the road to look when watching the balloon.
- Do not block narrow roads or driveways.
- Do not trespass.
- Do not climb fences.
- Do not enter locked gates.
- Do not sample crops.
- Keep chase vehicle on paved roads if possible; avoid raising dust on dirt roads.
- Leave gates as you found them.

Landing and Recovery

- Try to find landowner to ask permission to land and deflate.
- Do not drive into a field until you have permission or tried to get permission.
- Take only one vehicle to the landing site. Ask others politely not to enter.
- Drive carefully so you do not damage a field; drive along rows rather than across.
- Stay clear of equipment and machinery.
- Do not dally. Get balloon out immediately.
- Seek landowner if there is any crop or field damage.
- When possible, always tell the landowner "thank you."

FIGURE 2-2.—Balloon Ground Crew Information Sheet.

for the benefits of the event. In unknown territory, you should provide the chase crew with maps, and, if desired, a local person to act as guide.

A typical flight briefing may be "I intend to make a 1-hour flight and I have about 2 hours of fuel on board. From my weather briefing and the pibal, I should travel in a southeasterly direction, but if I go west I will land before getting to the freeway. I will probably do a lot of contour flying, but may go up to 2,000 feet to look around. Let's use channel one on the radio. There is a county road map on the front seat."

As stated before, the optimum size inflation crew for a sport balloon is four people—the pilot operating the burner, two people holding the mouth open, and one person on the crown line. Many pilots prefer a larger number of crewmembers; however, it is important to be aware that too many crewmembers may often be working against each other due to lack of coordination.

Pilot/Crew Communications

Radio communication between the balloon and the chase vehicle is fairly common. If you use radios, obey all Federal Communications Commission (FCC) regulations. Use call signs, proper language, and keep transmissions short. Many balloonists prefer not to use radios to communicate with their chase vehicle because it can be distracting to both pilot and chase vehicle driver. In any case, it is a good idea to agree on a common phone number before a flight in case the chase crew loses the balloon.

The crew is the pilot's ground representative to spectators, passengers, police, landowners, press, and anyone else who may have occasion to be interested in the balloon. The crew should always act responsibly because their actions reflect directly upon the pilot.

The pilot is responsible for all aspects of the flight. Crewmembers should follow instructions even if they have learned different techniques from other pilots. Do not assume anything, because different pilots may expect different things from their crew. Before the noise and momentum make discussion difficult, you should give the crew briefing and any requirements discussed with the pilot before inflation.

While it is desirable to have the chase crew present at the landing, the crew should remember the balloon pilot could land without assistance. The crew should not do anything dangerous or inconsiderate in an attempt to assist in the landing.

CHASE

Chase Crew

To begin with, a chase crew needs a reliable and suitable vehicle. Suggested items to carry might be a clock or wristwatch, maps and aeronautical charts, compass, binoculars, communications radio, and gifts for local people and landowners that may volunteer to help.

The chase crew may be one person or many. When offering seats in the chase vehicle, do not forget to leave room for all occupants of the balloon for the trip back.

Two people in the chase vehicle is best for a typical hot air balloon chase this allows for one to drive and one to watch. Chasing balloons is more watching and less driving, but it is nice to be able to separate the two jobs. Most of the time, the chase crew is parked alongside the road watching the balloon drift slowly toward them.

Pre-launch Considerations

The chase usually starts when the balloon leaves the ground, but there are preparations that must be made before inflation. For instance, the chase crew must have the keys to the chase vehicle. The last place the car keys should be is in the pocket of the balloon pilot, who is already in the air.

Another prelaunch consideration should be to get the chase vehicle clear of the launch site and ready to depart. Sometimes, the chase vehicle becomes trapped at the launch site because of spectators and vehicles blocking their way. At launch time, balloon watchers usually become enchanted and completely mesmerized by the beautiful balloons, oblivious to the efforts of the chase crews to get out and start chasing. In such situations, it is prudent to get the chase vehicle in position for the chase before the inflation begins.

Another consideration is for the pilot to remind the chase crew of the conditions and purposes of the flight. The crew does a better job if they know the approximate direction of the flight, maximum time in the air, possibility of multiple flights, known terrain hazards, and preferred landing sites. If the pilot forgets to give an appropriate briefing to the chase crew, the crew should ask. The best time to cover this briefing is before the inflation begins, as a checklist item.

Direction of Flight

The first element of the flight the chase crew must know is the direction the balloon is going. It is important to understand that the balloon's direction is very difficult to detect from a moving vehicle. Many pilots recommend that the chase crew drive the chase vehicle away from the launch site only far enough away to get the vehicle out of the way of the balloon (and other balloons) and to get clear of any possible spectator crowds. As soon as the crew is sure they are clear of other traffic, they should park in a suitable place, and with a good view of the balloon, determine the balloon's direction of flight. There is no point in rushing after the balloon until you know where it is going. The balloon changes direction shortly after launch if the winds aloft are different from the surface winds.

After a while the crew should proceed to a point estimated to be in the balloon's path. In other words, get in front of the balloon so it will fly over the chase vehicle. If the balloon is moving at 5 knots, the chase crew need only drive a short time to get in front of the balloon. The direction of flight is much easier to determine if the balloon is floating directly toward you rather than flying parallel to the vehicle's path.

If a radio is not being used, as the balloon flies over the chase vehicle, the pilot and crew can communicate by voice or with hand signals. In this instance the crew should be outside the vehicle with the engine turned off.

Use of a navigator with an appropriate map in the chase vehicle can be very helpful, especially during the early stages of the chase. The balloon may be flying a straight line, but the chase vehicle must follow roads. It is handy for the driver to have someone tell him or her when and where to turn.

Many pilots do not use radios because of the noise and distraction a radio can cause in the basket. However, in unfamiliar territory, where there are few roads, and near towered airports, a radio may be useful or even necessary.

Chase Crew Behavior

During the chase, remember to drive legally and politely. The chase crew is of no use to the pilot if the police stop them. A chase vehicle speeding around the countryside will unfavorably impress local residents. Speeding is bad for obvious reasons. Also, it is bad because it may give an impression of an emergency when none exists. Even if the chase vehicle is not painted like a circus wagon or advertising truck, local residents will soon put two and two together and figure out the person in the vehicle is chasing the balloon.

If possible, the chase crew should try to keep the chase vehicle in sight of the balloon. The pilot may be comforted to know the crew is nearby and not stuck in a ditch, or off somewhere changing a flat tire. When the vehicle is stopped at the side of the road, park it in the open so the entire vehicle is visible to the balloon pilot.

While chasing, the crew should observe all NO TRESPASSING and KEEP OUT signs, and stay on public, paved roads. Vehicular trespass is common and the laws are very restrictive regarding vehicles on private property. Pilots and their chase crews should adhere to local trespass laws.

The chase crew should not drive the chase vehicle into the landing field until permission has been received, or at least until the pilot and the crew are in agreement that it is okay to drive into the field. If the crew is unsure, it is better to walk into the field and consult with the pilot.

The chase crew is the pilot's personal representative on the ground. Any action taken by the chase crew reflects directly on the balloon pilot. Chasing a balloon is a lot of fun. Like flying, the better it is done, the more fun it is.

CHAPTER 3

INFLATION, LAUNCH, AND LANDING

This chapter introduces inflation, launch, and landing. It also provides useful information on landowner relations.

INFLATION

The inflation procedure takes the balloon envelope from a pile of fabric to a spheroid capable of lifting a load. The pilot's goal should be a smooth, controlled inflation that does not damage the environment, the balloon, or harm the crew. At the end of the inflation, the balloon should be upright, close to equilibrium, and ready to fly.

Historical Background

When the modern hot air balloon was being invented, one of the first pieces of inflation equipment was a relatively huge squirrel cage centrifugal blower—the type seen on roofs of old buildings. Because of its design, with the engine off to the side, and out of the airstream, this type of blower could be used to pump warm air into the envelope. A wand-type propane device, similar to present-day weed burners, heated the air. The flame was held in front of the blower inlet, thus air was heated prior to entry in the envelope.

Because the blower was noisy, bulky, expensive, and potentially dangerous, many early balloonists chose to do flap inflation. Two or three people would stand at the mouth of the balloon, with their backs to the basket. Each person would grasp the upper lip of the mouth with widely spaced hands. As the flappers moved the upper lip up and down in unison, the envelope would partially fill with ambient air.

A couple of other early inflators are worthy of comment. Some pilots, trying to avoid smelly, flammable gasoline, used electric fans. Automobile or truck radiator fans were tried, but their small size made inflation very slow. Another attempt was to attach radiator fan blades directly to an automotive starter motor, plugged into the chase vehicle battery. The motor drew so much power from the battery that the battery would die. The solution was to keep the vehicle engine running to keep the battery charged. The fan, however, was still essentially gasoline powered, polluted the air, and required the chase vehicle to be parked too close to the balloon.

Today most hot air balloons are inflated with commercially built or homemade gasoline-powered, propeller-bladed, inflation fans. Another type of fan you might see in use today is a small, propane-powered, 3-horse power (HP), aluminum-bladed, ducted, axial fan.

Inflation Style

There are many different styles of inflation. Some pilots use one or two large fans to inflate the balloon fast and get it tight. Some pilots prefer to fill the envelope slowly to give them time for preflight preparation. Some use many crewmembers, some use only a few crewmembers. Balloon size, available crew, weather, location, and personal preference are factors that determine procedures and number of crewmembers.

Typically, for an average balloon, an inflation crew of three is optimum, with the pilot at the burners and the other two people at the mouth. In windy or crowded situations, it is important to have a fourth person holding the crown line.

If inflation requires more crew than usual, due to the windy conditions, you should consider canceling the flight. Although the balloon may get airborne, chances are that flying out of your comfort zone and having to prepare for a very windy landing may impair concentration. The distraction may hinder safe, enjoyable flying.

Briefing to Crew and Passengers

Prior to the actual inflation, you should brief the crew and any passengers.

Crew Briefing

Whether this is the crewmembers' first time or one-hundredth time crewing, they should be briefed before each flight. Instructions contained in the briefing may be less detailed for an experienced crew. The following instructions should be given for each flight.

- The position and duties during inflation.
- The duties once the balloon has reached equilibrium.
- The estimated length of flight and any information that will aid the chase and recovery.

Passenger Briefing

Prior to inflation is the most appropriate time to give passengers their first briefing for behavior during the flight and landing. Inform them that during the landing they should stand in the basket where you indicate (based on wind conditions), facing the direction of flight, with feet and knees together, knees slightly bent, holding tightly to the sides of the basket. They are not to exit the basket until instructed to do so by you, the pilot.

The balloon is ready for inflation once the preflight preparation is complete. Equipment is stowed in the basket and in the chase vehicle. Park the chase vehicle upwind, out of the way in case of a wind change, with the keys in the ignition.

The Inflation

After the balloon is correctly laid out, place the inflation fan to the side of the burner within arm's reach of the pilot, facing into the center of the envelope mouth, making sure the fan blades are not in line with the pilot, crew, or spectators. If the fan is well designed and maintained, it will not move around and will not require constant attention during operation. Exact fan placement depends on the type of fan, burner, and size of the envelope. Pump air into the envelope and not under, over, or to the side of the mouth.

You should place one crewmember at each side of the mouth of the balloon to lift the mouth material and create an opening for air to enter the envelope. During cold inflation (i.e., with the fan only) hold the mouth open wide enough to admit air from the fan. Inflate the balloon to approximately 50 to 75 percent full of cold air.

At this point, you should check to see that control lines are correctly deployed, and that the deflation panel is correctly positioned. This can all be done through or in the vent or from the top; it is not necessary to walk on the fabric.

Once you complete the preflight inspection and are satisfied that the envelope contains enough ambient air to begin hot inflation, the two crewmembers at the mouth should hold the mouth open as wide and as tall as possible, to keep the fabric away from the burner flame. The crewmembers should face away from the burner. Before activating the blast valve, you should make eye contact with each crewmember at the mouth and make sure they are ready. Crew readiness is very important. The crew on the mouth of the envelope must be aware the burner is about to be used.

At this point, the fan has been facing into the center of the mouth. If the fan remains in this position, the burner flame will be distorted and bend toward a crewmember. Redirect the fan toward the nearest corner of the envelope mouth. With the fan directed parallel to the burner flame, there will be less distortion of the flame and less tendency for the air from the fan to bend the flame to one side.

The first burn or blast of the burner should be a short one to confirm the correct direction of the flame and to check the readiness of the mouth crew. If they are startled by the flame or noise and drop the fabric, the short burn will minimize damage.

Now that the fan is facing the correct direction, parallel to the burner flame, and the crew is ready, you can inflate the balloon. To minimize damage to the envelope and discomfort of the crew, inflate the balloon with a series of short burns and pauses, rather than one continuous blast. Inflate using standard burns, with short pauses of about 2 seconds between burns. The pauses give the fabric and skin a chance to cool and allow communication between you and the crew, if necessary. Under some circumstances, you will notice a contraction and inflation of the balloon mouth. You can easily time the burns to match the expansion of the mouth to avoid damaging the fabric during a contraction. These mouth movements are called breathing and burns should be timed to match the full open time. Later in this chapter the one-long-blast style is explained.

Allow the fan to run at a reduced speed until the balloon mouth lifts off the ground and is no longer receiving air. If the fan is turned off too soon, envelope air will come back out of the mouth and the backwash distorts the flame at the beginning and end of each blast. Do not hurry to turn off the fan.

The next step is to continue the burn-and-pause routine until the balloon is nearly ready to leave the ground. The crew should be standing by the basket ready to hold the balloon (hands on), in case you miscalculate and the balloon starts to lift off the ground before you are ready.

Many pilots fail to achieve equilibrium (see Glossary for definition) immediately after inflation. If equilibrium is not achieved, the balloon is much more susceptible to wind. For example, if the envelope is not full, a slight wind can cave in a side causing a spinnaker effect. If the balloon is erect, but not ready to fly, the pilot has only one option should the balloon start to move horizontally; the pilot must deflate. If the balloon is only 5 or 10 seconds of heat away from lifting off, the pilot has the choice of deflation or launch. In order to exercise the launch option, all equipment and passengers must be on board.

When inflating under variable wind conditions, in a confined area, or at a rally with other balloons, you should place a crewmember on the crown line to keep the envelope in line with the burner and to minimize rolling. If you have a person on the crown line, it should be someone of average size. If it takes more than one person to stabilize the balloon, it is probably too windy to fly.

The duty of the crown line crewmember is to hold the end of the line, lean away from the envelope, and use body weight to stabilize the envelope. This person must wear leather gloves, which provide a good grip on the line, and must never wrap the line around a wrist (or any other body part).

As the air is heated and the envelope starts to rise, the crewmember holding the crown line should allow the line to pull him towards the basket, putting resistance on the line to keep the envelope from swaying or moving too fast. Release the line slowly when the envelope is vertical.

The crown line varies in length. Some pilots let the line hang straight down; some pilots connect the end of the line to the basket or burner frame. Other pilots keep the line only long enough to assist with a windy inflation, or deflation in a confined area. Usually, there are no knots in the crown line, but you might find a type of loop attached to it. Some pilots put knots in their line, or attach flags or other objects. These may snag in trees and cause problems. Lines tied to the basket form a huge loop that may snag a tree limb and should be secured with a light, breakaway tie. Once the balloon is fully inflated and standing upright, at least one crewmember should stand near the basket to assist with passenger entry and to receive any last-minute instructions. Stow the fan and all other equipment in the chase vehicle and clear the area. Now the balloon is ready for launch.

Earlier in this chapter, it was stated that there are many different styles of inflation. The procedure described above is just one style.

Some pilots prefer to inflate the balloon with one-long-blast of the burner. The advantage of this type of inflation is that the balloon inflates a few seconds faster and the mouth tends to stay fully open during the process. There are several disadvantages. Voice communication is nearly impossible due to the noise of the burner. Anyone or anything within 6 feet of the burner may get burned. Also, some burners could be discolored or damaged by long burns. Properly used, a modern balloon burner should look like new and last a long time. Misused, a burner will discolor, warp, and leak.

Many pilots like to pack the balloon full of cold air using a large fan. This may make a tighter mouth, helping the pilot to avoid burning fabric, and the balloon may be less affected by a light wind when it is round and tight. However, if the balloon is filled with cold air, the actual hot inflation ~~will~~ take a little longer.

Another style used is tying-down or tying-off the balloon before a cold inflation. Some balloon event organizers require that the balloon be secured, usually due to limited space at the launch site or marginal wind conditions. Tying a balloon may not be an adequate solution for either situation; however, there may be occasions when a pilot is required to tie-off a balloon.

Every major balloon manufacturer specifies the approved method for tying off, but few have described an approved inflation tie-down system. Balloon baskets, suspensions, load plates, and burner supports have been destroyed by improper tie-off in light winds. If tying down for inflation is a must, ask the manufacturer of the balloon for instructions for inflation tie-down and use only the balloon manufacturer's recommended procedures and techniques.

The first requirement is to comply with factory recommendations for the tie-down system. The second requirement is to have something substantial to tie off to. This requirement is in direct conflict with the basic rule not to have obstacles near the balloon during inflation. Whatever the balloon is being tied to will probably be, or become, an obstacle. A wind change during inflation can turn an envelope into a chase vehicle cover. Being draped over a chase vehicle can be devastating to an envelope!

If the tie-off line is attached near the burners, the line becomes a restriction to the directions available for aiming the flame. As the envelope inflates and tries to stand erect, the restraining line can interfere with appropriate movement of the basket.

For an early morning flight, many pilots argue that, if the wind is so strong at launch time that you must tie-down, it is likely the wind will be even stronger at landing time. Therefore, it might not be prudent to take off when a high-wind landing is probable.

Some pilots state their preference for tying down at launch by explaining that they may have had a real problem and the balloon might have gotten away, if they had not tied down. Generally, in such cases, the real problem was continuing inflation in conditions that were too windy. If you must tie down, use the proper equipment, a strong release mechanism, an appropriate anchor, and remember that the tie-down line may be a danger when released under tension.

The inflation is the first action of ballooning that requires a pilot in command. The inflation should be safe and efficient. Now, the balloon is ready to fly.

LAUNCH

At this point, the balloon is just slightly heavier than equilibrium and ready to launch.

If carrying passengers, now is the time to invite them in the basket. Immediately compensate for the additional weight with sufficient heat to regain equilibrium. The passengers have already been briefed on the correct landing procedure. Now is the time to again brief them on behavior in the basket; advise them not to touch any control lines, to take care of their possessions, to stay well within the confines of the basket, not to sit on the side of the basket, and, above all, to obey the pilot in command.

At least one crewmember should remain near the basket in case the pilot or passengers need assistance. This is a good time to give the crew a final briefing regarding the expected distance and length of the flight. If other balloons are launching from the same area, ask a crewmember to step back from the balloon to check that it is clear above.

Two or three standard burns in a row from equilibrium usually provides a slow departure from the ground. If there are no nearby, downwind obstacles to clear, a slow ascent rate is preferred to test wind direction and detect subtle wind changes. Climbing at a slow rate is the best way to avoid running into balloons above. Although the balloon below has the right-of-way (due to lack of visibility above), the higher balloon needs time to climb out of the way, if necessary.

A fast ascent rate from launch is only to avoid ground obstacles or to pass quickly through an adverse wind, and only when it is clear above.

It is very easy to be distracted during launch and make an unintentional descent. Make sure all ground business is taken care of, such as instructing the chase crew and stowing all equipment correctly, before leaving the ground.

Be aware of the possibility of uncontrolled lift (oftentimes referred to as *false lift*), and the possibility of an unplanned descent caused by surface wind or an ascent from a sheltered launch site. Pay attention to obstacles, including the chase vehicle, fences, and particularly to powerlines. Realize where all powerlines are and visually locate them as soon as possible.

Some organized events have a maximum ascent and descent rate of 200 to 300 FPM. However, in the case of a problem, the pilot in command is ultimately responsible and, if safety requires, may have to exceed event-set limits. Instructions from an event director or launch director never supersede your responsibility as pilot in command of an aircraft.

Return flights in a balloon are fun and more rare than they should be. If you would like to make a return flight, your chances will increased if you start your flight moving toward the upwind direction. If possible, when the winds are variable, fly the early part of the flight in a direction other than the normal prevailing direction. Then the second half of the flight can be in the normal direction, which may take the balloon back to the launch site.

Now, at the beginning of your flight, is the time to learn about wind directions at different elevations and to start planning the flight direction and landing site.

APPROACH TO LANDING

No other aircraft has as many different types of landings as a balloon. Most aircraft, including gliders and helicopters, land on relatively smooth, hard places. Balloons rarely land on smooth, hard places. Since the balloon is stronger than people are and less susceptible to damage, a soft landing is one that is judged to be easy on the passengers.

Birds are probably the only flying things that have more available landing sites. Balloons can land safely in places that most other aircraft cannot. Balloons can land on the ground or in the water, on the flat or side of a hill, in bushes or trees (with maybe a little damage), on plowed and irrigated fields, in snow or mud. There is an infinite variety of suitable balloon landing sites and rarely are two balloon landings alike.

When a landing site is being considered, you should first think about the suitability of the site. "Is it safe, is it legal, and is it polite?" When considering surface winds, you should make certain there is adequate access to the site with respect to obstructions.

Some Basic Rules of Landing

The final, safe resting place of the balloon is a major consideration in landing. Making a soft landing is not as important as getting the balloon where you want it. Having an easy retrieval is not as important as an accident-free, appropriate landing site.

Plan the landing early enough so that fuel quantity is not a distraction. Plan on landing with enough fuel so that even if your first approach to a landing site is unsuccessful, there is enough fuel to make a couple more approaches.

The best landing site is one that is bigger than you need and has alternatives. If you have three prospective sites in front of you, aim for the one in the middle in case your surface wind estimate was off. If you have multiple prospective landing sites in a row along your path, take the first one and save the others for a miscalculation. Unless there is a 180° turn available, all the landing sites behind are lost.

The best altitude for landing is the lowest altitude. Anyone can land from 1 foot above the ground; it takes skill to land from 100 feet.

A low approach, assuming no obstacles, gives you the slowest touchdown speed because the winds are usually lightest close to the ground.

It is usually better to fly over an obstacle and land beyond it than to land in front of it. Overfly powerlines, trees, and water, among other obstacles, on the way to the landing, rather than attempting to land in front of them and risk being dragged into them.

Before beginning your approach, plan to fly a reasonable descent path to the landing site, using the step-down approach method, the low (shallow) approach method, or a combination of the two. [Figure 3-1]

Step-Down Approach

The step-down approach method involves varying descent rates. This procedure is used to determine lower level wind velocities and directions so that options may be considered until beginning the final descent phase to landing. There are other methods to evaluate lower level wind conditions, such as dropping strips of paper, etc., or small balloons. While the descent path can be varied and sometimes may be quite shallow, it is important to avoid long, level flight segments below minimum safe altitudes without intending to land. Level flight at low altitudes could lead an observer to believe that you have discontinued the approach and established level flight at less than a minimum safe altitude.

FIGURE 3-1.—Step-down approach and low (shallow) approach.

Low Approach

The second type of approach is a low or shallow approach. If there are no obstacles between the balloon and the proposed landing site, a low or shallow approach allows you to check the wind closer to the surface. Also, the closer you are to the surface, the easier it is to land.

Obstacles

If there is an obstacle between the balloon and the landing site, the following are the three safe choices.

1. Give the obstacle appropriate clearance and drop in from altitude.
2. Reject the landing and look for another site to land.
3. Fly a low approach to the obstacle, fly over the obstacle allowing plenty of room, and then make the landing.

The first choice is the most difficult, requiring landing from a high approach and then a fast descent at low altitude. The second choice is the most conservative, but may not be available if you are approaching your last landing site. The third choice is preferable. Flying toward the site at low altitude provides an opportunity to check the surface winds. By clearing the obstacle while ascending—always the safest option—you will end up with a short, but not too high, approach.

The advantage of a low approach is apparent in situations where, when you get the balloon close to the ground, you find the wind direction is different from what you had assumed or planned. If you have started your approach, some distance from your landing target, you may have time to climb back to the wind that takes you in the desired direction and still have a chance to make your original target. In some cases, finding out too late that there is an adverse wind near the surface makes the planned landing impossible. This type of approach requires more skill in order to avoid overcorrecting.

Congested Areas

Making an approach in a congested area, and subsequently discovering the site to be impossible or inappropriate, is another example of possibly being falsely accused of low flying. There are some inconsiderate pilots who fly too low in congested areas without reason, but they are rare. Every pilot will have an aborted landing situation occasionally. According to 14 CFR part 91, section 91.119 you may fly closer to the ground than the minimum altitude, if necessary for landing. For example, during your approach, the balloon turns away from the obviously preferred landing site, but there is another possible site only one-half mile in the proper direction. You have two choices: (1) go back up to a legal altitude and try again, or (2) stay low, in the wind you are sure will carry you to a good site, and try to make the second landing site.

In making the first choice, you could be accused of intentionally flying too low. However, with the second choice, you will fly lower for a longer period of time, which might appear to be a violation of the minimum altitude regulation. This is not an argument in favor of either technique. Many pilots prefer the second choice on the "once you go down to land, you had better land" theory.

Landing Techniques

Landing is probably the most demanding maneuver in ballooning. You must visualize your landing. Imagine the path through the air and across the ground. Look for obstacles, especially powerlines, near the imagined track. Note surface wind velocity and direction by looking for smoke, dust, flags, moving trees, and anything else that indicates wind direction. Do not be influenced too much by a wind indicator at a distance from the proposed site if there is a good indicator closer.

Visualize the descent to the site. For example, imagine you are flying level at 700 feet above ground level (AGL) and it is time to land. Checking the fuel, you have 30 percent remaining in two 20-gallon tanks. Your track across the ground is toward the southeast, but you observe a farmer's tractor making a column of dust that is traveling nearly due east. The dust cloud rises from the ground at about a 45° angle. From this information you can guess that the balloon will turn left as it descends. This means you are looking to the left of the line the balloon now travels. By dropping small tissue balls, you determine that the wind changes about halfway to the ground and continues to turn left about 45°. Visualize your descent being no faster than about 500 FPM initially and slowing to about 300 FPM about 400 feet AGL where you expect the turn will start. Because the balloon will lose some lift from the cooling effect of the wind direction change, plan on closely monitoring your descent during the turn.

With this imagined descent in mind, search for an appropriate landing site. The next fallow field to the left of your present path is blocked by tall powerlines. You reject the site.

The next field that seems appropriate is an unfenced grain stubble field bordered by dirt roads with a 30 foot-high powerline turning along the west side, to the left and parallel to your present track. You must cross over the powerlines to reach your proposed landing field. Under the powerlines is a paved road, with a row-crop of sugar beets to the right and directly in your present path.

You select as your landing target the intersection of the two dirt roads at the southeast corner of the field. Your planned path would be across the field diagonally giving the greatest distance from the powerlines. Extending the final approach line back over the powerlines and into the sugar beet field, select a target for your surface wind turn. Next, set the spot where you will begin the initial descent.

Now, reverse the procedure and perform the descent, turn, and landing that you visualized. If all goes as visualized, allow the balloon to cool and accelerate to about 500 FPM. Apply some heat to arrest the descent as you approach your imagined turning point over the beets; level off (or maybe actually climb a bit) as you cross over the powerlines (about 200 feet above them); allow the balloon to cool again as you set up another descent across the stubble field. Due to the 7 miles per hour (MPH) estimated wind, allow the basket to touch down about 150 feet out from the dirt road intersection to lose some momentum as the basket bounces and skids over to the road, just where you planned.

Imagine now, how the landing might have occurred not knowing the surface wind was different from the flightpath. Maybe the less considerate pilot would plan on landing in the beets. Maybe the crop will not be hurt and the farmer will not care. Unfortunately, the balloon turns unexpectedly toward the powerlines, causing the pilot to make several burns of undetermined amount, setting up a climb that prevents the pilot from landing on the dirt road. The road is right in line with the balloon's track, but disappearing behind the balloon. Another good landing site becomes unusable because of the lack of planning.

The thoughtful pilot makes a nice landing on a dirt road with 25 percent fuel remaining, while the unprepared pilot dives, turns, climbs, and is now back at 600 feet in the air looking for another landing site. For the next attempt, the pilot will have less fuel and be under more pressure, all because of not noticing the powerlines to the left and not checking the wind on the ground before making the descent. The first pilot visualized a plan, executed the plan, and is safely on the ground while the second pilot is saying, "Well, let's go down again and see what happens."

Do not have a "let's see what happens" attitude. Have a plan.

Practice Approaches

Approaching from a relatively high altitude, with a high descent rate, down to a soft landing, is a very good maneuver to practice. This is used when landing over an obstacle when maneuvering to your selected field is only possible from a higher than desired altitude. This maneuver can also be used when, due to inattention or distractions, you find yourself at a relatively high altitude approaching the last appropriate landing site. Practicing this type of approach should take place in an uninhabited area, and the obstacle should be a simulated obstacle.

A drop in landing or steep approach to landing is another good maneuver to practice. Being able to perform this maneuver can get you into that perfect field that is just beyond the trees, or just the other side of the orchard. Being able to drop quickly, but softly, into the fallow field between crops is more neighborly than making a low approach over the orchard. Being able to avoid frightening cattle or other animals during an approach is a valuable skill.

Having the skills to predict your track during the landing approach, touching down on your landing target, and stopping the balloon basket in the preferred place, can be very satisfying. It requires a sharp eye trained to spotting the indicators of wind direction on the ground.
Dropping bits of tissue, observing other balloons, smoke, steam, dust, and tree movement are all ways to predict the balloon track on its way to the landing site. Your most important observation is watching for powerlines.

A good approach usually earns a good landing. In ballooning, approaches can be practiced more often than landings.

Passenger Management

Prior to landing, you should explain correct posture and procedure to the passengers. Many balloon landings are gentle, stand-up landings. However, always prepare your passengers for the possibility of a hard impact. Instruct passengers to do the following.

- Stand in the appropriate area of the basket.
- Face the direction of travel.
- Place feet and knees together, with knees bent.
- Hold on tight in two places.
- Stay in the basket.

Stand in the appropriate area of the basket

Passengers and pilot should position themselves toward the rear of the basket. This accomplishes three things.

1. The leading edge of the basket is lifted as the floor tilts from the occupant weight shift, so the basket is less likely to dig into the ground and make a premature tip-over.
2. With the occupants in the rear of the basket and the floor tilted, the basket is more likely to slide along the ground and lose some speed before tipping.
3. The passengers are less likely to fall out of the front of the basket.

In a high-wind landing, passengers should stand in the front of the basket. The reason for this is so that, when the basket makes surface contact and tips over, passengers will fall a shorter distance and will not be pitched forward. They will be more likely to remain in the basket, minimizing the risk of injury.

Face the direction of travel

Feet, hips, and shoulders should be perpendicular to the direction of flight. Impact with the ground while facing to the side puts a sideways strain on the knees and hips, which do not naturally bend that way. Facing the opposite direction is more appropriate under certain conditions.

Place feet and knees together, with knees bent

To some people this may not seem to be a natural ready position; however, it is very appropriate to ballooning. The feet and knees together stance allows maximum flexibility. With the knees bent, one can use the legs as springs or shock absorbers in all four directions. With the feet apart, sideways flexibility is limited and knees do not like being bent to the side. With legs apart fore and aft, one foot in front of the other, there is the possibility of doing the splits and a likelihood of locking the front knee. Avoid using the word *brace* as in *brace yourselves*; it sounds as if knees should be locked or muscles tensed. Legs should be flexible and springy at landing impact.

Hold on tight in two places

This is probably the least followed of the landing instructions. Up to this point, the typical balloon flight has been relatively gentle and most passengers do not realize the shock that can occur when a 7,000-pound balloon contacts the ground. Urge your passengers to hold on tight. You should advise your passengers of correct places to hold on, whether they are factory-built passenger handles, or places in your basket you consider appropriate. The pilot must obey his or her own directions and also hold on firmly.

Stay in the basket

Some passengers, believing the flight is over as soon as the basket makes contact with the ground, will start to get out. Even a small amount of wind may cause the basket to bounce and slide after initial touchdown. If a 200-pound passenger decides to exit the basket at this point, the balloon will immediately begin to ascend. Everybody, including the pilot, should stay in the basket until it stops moving.

Monitoring of passengers is important because, after the balloon first touches down, passengers may forget everything they have been told. A typical response is for the passenger to place one foot in front of the other and lock the knee. This is a very bad position as the locked knee is unstable and subject to damage. Pilots should observe their passengers and order "feet together," "front (back) of the basket," "knees bent," "hold on tight," and "do not get out until I tell you!" The pilot should be a good example to passengers by assuming the correct landing position. Otherwise, passengers may think, "If the pilot does not do it, why should we."

It is very important that the passenger briefing be given more than once. Some balloon ride companies send an agreement to their passengers in advance, which includes the landing instructions. Passengers are asked to sign a statement that they have reviewed, read, and understand the landing procedure. Many pilots give passengers a briefing and landing stance demonstration on the ground before the flight. This briefing should be given again as soon as the pilot has decided to land.

The pilot is very busy during the landing watching the passenger's actions and reactions, closing fuel valves, draining fuel lines, cooling the burners, and deflating the envelope. The better the passengers understand the importance of the landing procedure, the better the pilot will perform these duties and make a safe landing.

LANDING

Landing Procedure Variations

Landing in tall bushes or trees requires that everyone turn around and face the rear to protect their faces and eyes from branches and twigs. All the other elements of the standard briefing remain the same.

Landing on a very steep side of a hill or side approach to a cliff requires that everybody get lower in the basket to avoid being tipped-out when the basket floor becomes parallel to the hillside or cliff. In a sidehill or downhill landing, being tipped-out of the basket becomes more likely.

Landing in water requires modification to the passenger briefing. In a ditching, make sure the passengers get clear of the basket in case it inverts due to fuel tank placement. Advise the passengers to keep a strong grip on the basket because it becomes a flotation device. Predicting the final disposition of the basket in water is difficult. If the envelope is deflated, you can expect the envelope to sink, as it is heavier than water. Fuel tanks will float because they are lighter than water, even when full. If the envelope retains air, and depending on fuel-tank configuration, the balloon may come to rest, at least for a while, on its side.

In general, a rattan basket offers protection, except in water, and everybody should stay inside the basket.

High-wind Landing

As soon as you know, explain to your passengers that a high-wind landing will follow. It is better to alert them than to allow them to be too casual. Brief your passengers on the correct posture and procedure for a high-wind landing, to include wearing gloves and helmets, if available or required.

Fly at the lowest safe altitude to a large field. Check that the deflation line is clear and ready. Avoid all obstacles, and make a low approach to the near edge of the field. When committed to the landing, brief passengers again, turn off fuel valves, drain fuel lines, and turn off pilot lights.

Depending on the landing speed and surface, open the deflation vent at the appropriate time to control ground travel. Monitor your passengers, making sure they are properly positioned in the basket and holding on tightly.

Deflate the envelope and monitor it until all the air is exhausted. Be alert for fire, check your passengers, and prepare for recovery.

Landing Considerations

When selecting a landing site, three considerations, in order of importance, are safety of passengers, and persons and property on the ground; landowner relations; and ease of recovery.

Following are some questions you should ask when evaluating a landing site.

- Is it a safe place for my passengers and the balloon?
- Would my landing create any hazard for any person or property on the ground?
- Will my presence create any problems (noise, startling animals, etc.) for the landowner?

The last and least important consideration is recovery. Many pilots rank ease of recovery too high, and create enemies of landowners and residents. Convenience for the pilot and crew are less important than other considerations, which have longer-lasting effects.

Crew Responsibilities

The policy regarding expectations of crew help at landing is—if you cannot land the balloon without help, you should not be flying. It is not always possible for the chase crew to be at the landing site, so plan to land without assistance.

If the crew is at the landing site and clearly able to render assistance, you have options. Have the crew pull the balloon across a field to the road while it is still inflated or gently lead the inflated balloon away from any possible obstacles.

The crew is of no help in a windy landing. Crew will only be of assistance after the basket has stopped moving. There is a possibility of people on the ground being injured while trying to assist with a windy landing—even a moderately windy landing. Remember that a 77,000 cubic foot balloon has a momentum weight of several tons. Do not ever get in front of a moving balloon basket.

Deploying a drop line is useful only if the crew is strong, healthy, trained, and wearing gloves. Rarely should a pilot ask a stranger for assistance during landing. Use great care with a drop line, or handling line and use only in very light or calm winds.

Injuries in ballooning are few, and most happen during landing. If you are carrying passengers, your goal is to provide them with the gentlest landing possible in the best possible site. When flying alone, practice landings so you know how to control your balloon at the end of the flight.

Maintaining Good Relations With Landowners

The greatest threat to the continued growth of ballooning is poor landowner relations. The emphasis should be to create and maintain good relations with those who own and work the land that balloonists fly over and land on. Balloon pilots must never forget that at most landing sites, they are unexpected visitors.

An assuming balloonist may think the uninvited visit of a balloon is a great gift to individuals on the ground. The balloon pilot may not know the difference between a valuable farm crop and uncultivated land. A balloonist may not notice the grazing cattle. A chase vehicle driver may drive fast down a dirt road raising unnecessary dust. A crewmember may trample a valuable crop.

There are several situations where a balloon pilot or crew may anger the public. When people are angered, they demand action from the local police, county sheriff, FAA, or an attorney. The FAA does not initiate an investigation without a complaint. The balloonist is the one who initiates the landowner relation's problem.

How can balloonists ease the effect they have on people on the ground? First, develop your skills to allow yourself the widest possible choices of landing sites. If you fly in farmland, as many balloonists do, wear what is customary for the area. Make sure your crew is trained to respect the land, obey traffic laws, and be polite to everyone they come in contact with. The crew should always get permission for the balloon to land and the chase vehicle to enter private property.

You should learn the trespass laws of your home area. You should be able to find them at the library. In some states, it is very difficult for the balloon pilot and passengers to trespass, but very easy for the chase vehicle and crew to trespass.

If you land on the wrong side of a locked gate or fence, the first thing your chase crew should do is try to find the landowner or resident to get permission to enter. If no one can be found, it may be necessary to carry the balloon and lift it over the fence.

Do not cut or knock down fences, as it will probably be considered trespassing. In some places, even the possession of fence-cutting and fence-repairing tools may be interpreted as possession of burglary tools, creating liabilities. Pilot and crew should have a clear understanding of what is acceptable and what is not acceptable.

Sometimes local law enforcement people will arrive at the scene of a balloon-landing site. Someone may have called them or they may have seen the balloon in the air. They may just be interested in watching the balloon (which is usually the case), or they may think a legal violation has occurred. If law enforcement people approach you, always be polite. They probably do not know much about federal law regarding aviation. However, even if they are wrong and you know they are wrong, there is no point in antagonizing them with a belligerent attitude. It is better to listen than to end up in court.

Chase crews should always be friendly to farm workers and other local workers. The person you waved to last week may be the tractor driver who pulls your chase vehicle out of a muddy rut next week.

Figure 3-2 is suggested information pilots should give to all crewmembers titled, *Landowner Relations Information Sheet*. Keep copies in your chase vehicle and go over them with all crewmembers, including pickup crew at events.

One of your most important concerns is landowner relations. The continued availability of balloon landing sites depends on good landowner and public relations. Constant vigilance by balloon pilots and crews to do no harm to the land and be considerate of people and property on the ground is a must.

LANDOWNER RELATIONS INFORMATION SHEET

Overview

These procedures, for use by balloon pilots, students, and crews, were developed over many years and are standard operating procedures for many balloon operators.

While you can control the launch site, you cannot always control the flightpath and landing site. Many times a balloon pilot is an uninvited guest. Sometimes the pilot, crew, or balloon is unwelcome.

Each pilot should develop the attitude, techniques, and skills which minimize or eliminate negative landowner relations. A balloon pilot should not use lack of experience, bad luck, or the weather, as an excuse for creating poor landowner relations.

Flight Elements

- **Skill and experience**—Pilots should practice flying skills to allow selection of appropriate landing sites. A skilled pilot is able to choose correct landing sites. Good landings (at appropriate sites) are the result of good skills and good decisions.
- **Knowledge of area**—Pilot and crew must know where balloons are welcomed and where they are not. Pilot and crew must know what crops grow when and where and what animals to avoid. When flying in a new area, the pilot should consult a local person, preferably a balloonist, for area information.
- **Purpose of flight**—Avoid flight in marginal conditions even if the flight is made for compensation or prizes. Resist peer pressure to fly at public events if conditions do not suit the pilot's skill and experience level. All operations, whether for fun or profit, must be considerate, legal, and safe.
- **Permission to use launch/landing site**—Do not assume a launch or landing site is available because another balloonist uses it or it is public property. If permission is required, obtain it and renew permission on a regular basis. When flying at any airport, know the rules (both on the ground and in the air) and obey them.
- **Crew briefing**—The crew is the pilot's representative on the ground and should be properly instructed.
- **Flight**—Low flying can annoy persons on the ground and frighten animals. Know the minimum altitude rules and obey them. If necessary, increase your altitude over sensitive areas. The CFRs are only the minimum; animals, for instance, may require more clearance. While the balloon is in flight, the chase crew should not drive too fast, make dust, block traffic, anger motorists, or create a feeling of emergency. Crews should be polite on the road and pilots considerate in the air. Do not do anything that could be offensive to the landowner, whether verbal or nonverbal.
- **Common sense**—Landowners must be treated with respect. Costumes and strange clothing interfere with landowner relations. The best attire to wear is what residents of the area wear. Thank the landowners for the use of their property, and let them know you are grateful.
- **General behavior**—Do not litter. Clean up launch and landing sites. Do not raise dust or disturb animals. Do not pick crops or remove anything. Obey NO TRESPASSING signs. Be pleasant to everyone; treat them with respect. Wave to drivers of other vehicles. When you meet a landowner, representative, farmer, or worker, always introduce yourself. Offer your hand, give your name, and say "Thank you."
- **Emergency landing**—In a real emergency, land as soon as it is safe. Do not abuse the emergency excuse. Do not claim an emergency when it is not. Use the term *emergency* carefully; an FAA/NTSB report may be required.
- **FAA concerns**—The FAA is seldom concerned over where a balloon launches or lands, unless there is a complaint, reported accident, or possibility of pilot negligence. Know the regulations and obey them. The FAA's duty is to promote air safety and protect people on the ground.

FIGURE 3-2.—Landowner relations information sheet.

CHAPTER 4

INFLIGHT MANEUVERS

This chapter discusses various aspects of inflight maneuvers. It covers the standard burn, level flight, ascents and descents, horizontal control, and contour flying. Also, included is an introduction to radio communications.

STANDARD BURN

Balloon pilots have few outside sources, instruments, or gauges to help them fly. When a balloon pilot uses the burner, there is no way of knowing exactly how much lift will be increased. The pyrometer tells the approximate temperature of the air surrounding the instrument's sensor, but there is no indicator or gauge to tell what the effect is on the balloon.

There are few standards in ballooning and very little are calibrated. There is little to help the balloon pilot determine how much heat is being put into the envelope. There is no gauge or dial that calibrates the number of British thermal units (Btu) that have been added to the hot air gathered above. Because there are few mechanical aids to help balloon pilots fly, some ways must be created to standardize operations so the outcome of certain actions are predictable and the balloon is controllable.

To fly with precision, the balloon pilot needs to know how much heat is going into the envelope at any given time and what that heat will do. The standard burn is one way to gauge in advance the balloon's reaction to the use of the burner.

The standard burn is an attempt to calibrate the heat being used. If each burn can be made identical, the balloon pilot can think and plan, in terms of number of burns, rather than just using random, variable amounts of heat with an unknown effect.

The standard burn is based on using the blast valve or trigger valve found on most balloon burners. Some brands use a valve that requires only a fraction of an inch of movement between closed and open, and some require moving the blast valve handle 90°. While the amount of motion required to change the valve from fully closed to fully open varies; the principle remains the same. Try to make burns that are identical to each other.

A standard burn could be approximately 3 to 5 seconds long, depending upon the size of the envelope, condition of the envelope, and experience level of the pilot. The burn begins with the brisk, complete opening of the blast valve and ends with the brisk, complete closing of the valve at the end of the burn. Some pilots, during their training, count "one-one thousand, two-one thousand, three-one thousand," to develop the timing.

The standard burn does not mean a burn that is standard between pilots, but rather, it is an attempt for the individual pilot to make all burns exactly the same length. The goal is not only to make each burn of exactly the same length, but also to make each burn exactly the same. Therefore, the pilot must open and close the valve exactly the same way each time. Most balloon burners were designed to operate with the blast valve fully open for short periods of time. When the blast valve is only partially opened, two things happen, (1) the burner is not operating at full efficiency, and (2) the pilot is not sure how much heat is being generated. A partially opened valve is producing a fraction of the heat available, but there is no way of knowing what the fraction is.

Another advantage of briskly opening and closing the valve is to minimize the amount of time you have a yellow, soft flame. During inflation, for instance, a strong, narrow, pointed flame that goes into the mouth opening, without overheating the mouth fabric or crew, is desirable. A partial-throttle flame is wide and short, and subject to distortion by wind or the inflation fan. If less than a full burn is desired, shorten the time the valve is open, not the amount the valve is open. Due to burner design (and the inefficiency of a partially opened valve), three 1-second burns will not produce as much heat as one 3-second burn.

A pilot using evenly spaced, identical burns appears to be decisive and precise. There is something professional and experienced about the even rhythm of using standard burns.

Another advantage of evenly spaced, identical burns is passenger comfort. The noise of the burner sometimes startles passengers. When not using the burner, pilots should keep their hands away from the blast valve handle. Then, when they raise their hand to operate the blast valve handle, passengers will know what to expect and will not be surprised or startled by a noise without warning. Passengers soon become accustomed to the rhythm of the standard burn.

Using the standard burn, pilots can better predict the effect of each burn, use the burner and fuel more efficiently, and have a better flame pattern. The standard burn will be referred to when discussing specific maneuvers.

Flying by the numbers as described in this chapter is not a goal in itself, but a mechanical tool to develop smoothness and consistency. If the mechanical aspects of flying can be learned, that systematic cadence can then be converted into a rhythm that is smooth and polished. With practice, the rhythm will become second nature and pilots will fly with smooth precision, without thinking about it.

Enjoyment is greatly enhanced when a pilot can fly almost automatically, without using a great deal of concentration. This does not mean that the pilot should try to achieve thoughtless flying, but should reach a stage where relaxation is possible and enjoying the flight comes naturally.

Developing your own standard burn, and knowing that a given number of burns achieves a desired result, enhances the pleasure you derive from flying. Also, added flight experience causes greater confidence.

LEVEL FLIGHT

Level flight is achieved when lift equals gravity. For all practical purposes, gravity is constant as far as the balloonist is concerned. The heated air trapped in the balloon envelope overcoming gravity creates buoyancy.

Equilibrium is achieved when lift exactly matches gravity and the balloon neither ascends nor descends, but remains at one altitude. Theoretically, equilibrium aloft is level flight, because the wind may raise or lower the balloon and the ambient air temperature is constantly changing.

Since it is the difference between ambient and envelope temperature that gives the balloon lift, the difference is really what a balloon pilot is interested in knowing, but few balloons have a temperature differential gauge.

In addition to fuel gauges, regulations require all hot air balloons to have an envelope temperature indicator, a rate-of-climb or vertical speed indicator (VSI), and an altimeter. The envelope temperature gauge helps prevent overheating and damage to the fabric. All balloon manufacturers have established maximum envelope temperatures that should not be exceeded. The VSI is a trend indicator showing the balloon's tendency to ascend or descend. A mechanical VSI will lag behind while an electronic VSI is more sensitive. An altimeter is similar. A mechanical altimeter lags behind and a digital altimeter is very sensitive.

Since the air around the balloon is constantly moving and changing temperature, instruments lag. The human eye is the best gauge for determining if a balloon at low altitude is ascending, flying level, or descending.

Theoretically, if a pilot were to hold a hot air balloon at a constant temperature, the balloon would float at a constant altitude. However, there is no practical way to hold the envelope air temperature constant. When the first modern hot air balloons were flown, pilots used a metering valve to adjust precisely a constant flame, hoping to hold the balloon in level flight. Anyone who has tried to fly that way has found the technique is noisy, fuel inefficient, damaging to the burners, and nearly impossible. Most modern hot air balloons are flown with a blast valve using unregulated tank pressure.

For every altitude there is an equilibrium temperature. If a pilot is flying at 500 feet mean sea level (MSL) and wants to climb to 1,000 feet MSL, the balloon temperature must be increased. This is not only to attain equilibrium at the new (higher) altitude, but some excess temperature must also be created to overcome inertia and get the balloon moving. Newton's law states, "A body at rest tends to stay at rest, and a body in motion tends to stay in motion."

A pilot flies level with a series of standard burns. Ideally, if the burns were of identical length and perfectly spaced, the balloon would hold a nearly constant altitude. The word *nearly* is used because the ambient air temperature is always changing. Each time a pilot burns, the balloon will tend to climb, but the air in the envelope is always trying to cool and the balloon will tend to descend. If the subsequent burns are perfectly timed, the balloon will fly in a series of very shallow sine waves.

An interesting experiment is to use the second hand of a wristwatch to establish a usable level flight pattern. Establish a standard burn and count how many burns are necessary to hold the balloon relatively level for 5 minutes. Assume you make five burns in 5 minutes and the balloon stays pretty much at 1,500 feet AGL. That means if you make a standard burn every 60 seconds, the balloon will fly level. Now you have a basis for controlling the balloon.

Of course, any variable will change the balloon flight. A heavier basket load, higher ambient temperature, or cloudy day, will all require more fuel (by shortening the interval between burns) to maintain level flight.

By experimenting, you can establish standards that can be used as a basis for all flights. On a hotter day, or with a heavier load, you could make the interval 55 seconds. A standard baseline to work from will then have been established.

With practice and using the second hand of a wristwatch, a new pilot can fly almost level. The exercise of trying to learn the pattern of burns (each day and hour is different) is an interesting training exercise, but not a practical real-life technique. The ability to hold a hot air balloon at a given altitude for any length of time is a skill that comes only with serious practice.

Level flight is probably the most important of all flight maneuvers. Nearly all other flight maneuvers are based on level flight. Level flight is very important to the student pilot aspiring to pass the practical test. Maintaining level flight is one of the few balloon maneuvers for which pass/fail tolerances have been established.

Unfortunately, most pilots do not spend enough time practicing level flight. If, during the practical test, you have a choice of altitudes, pick a lower, rather than higher altitude, to perform level flight. There are more visual references to assist in maintaining level flight when you are closer to the ground. Of course, you do not want to fly below minimum safe altitudes, and you should always be alert for powerlines along your flightpath.

Level flight is the basis of most other flight maneuvers. Evenly spaced, standard burns can produce smooth, relaxing level flight. The ability to fly straight and level comes with experience and practice.

USE OF INSTRUMENTS

Title 14 of the Code of Federal Regulations (14 CFR) part 31 and the balloon manufacturers' equipment lists specify certain instruments in the balloon. [Refer to appendix C] However, most pilots find they use instruments less and less as they gain experience and familiarity with the balloon.

For instance, while the VSI and the altimeter can be used to execute a smooth descent and transition to level flight, the experienced pilot will refer only occasionally to the instruments during maneuvers. This is especially so in maneuvers involving descents where they rely more on sight pictures and visual references.

Some beginning pilots become fixated on the instruments and forget to scan outside for obstacles. If a pilot spends too much time looking at the flight instruments, the instructor may cover the instrument pack with a spare glove or a hand to try to break the formation of a bad habit. Instruments are required and useful, but should not distract you from searching for obstacles. Always practice see and avoid.

ASCENTS AND DESCENTS

The temperature of the air inside the envelope controls balloon altitude. A balloon that is neither ascending nor descending is in equilibrium. To make the balloon ascend, increase the temperature of the air inside the envelope. If the temperature is increased just a little, the balloon seeks an altitude only a little higher and/or climb at a very slow rate. If the temperature is increased a lot, the balloon seeks a much higher altitude and/or climbs faster. If the balloon is allowed to cool, or hot air is vented, the balloon descends.

Ascents

Using evenly-spaced, identical standard burns to fly level, a pilot needs to only make two burns in a row to have added excess heat to make the balloon climb. For instance, if you can fly level with a standard burn every 60 seconds, and then make two burns instead of one, the balloon will have an extra burn and will climb. How fast the balloon will climb depends on how much extra heat you add. Under average conditions, if you make the standard burn to hold the balloon at level flight and immediately (not waiting the 60 seconds) you make a second burn, the average balloon will start a slow climb. Three burns in a row will result in a faster climb.

To avoid subjecting the burners and the envelope to the shock of a too-long burn, make two burns with a pause between burns. If a rapid ascent is desired, make three or maybe even four burns in a row, but always with a 5-second pause between burns to allow the heater to cool. The exception to this procedure is when using a double burner; in this case, alternate burners and wait only about 1 second between burns.

Once the desired climb rate is established, go back to the level flight routine to hold the balloon at that rate. The higher the altitude, or the faster the rate-of-climb, the shorter the interval between burns. In an average size balloon at 5,000 feet, the pilot may be required to make a standard burn every 15 to 20 seconds to keep the balloon climbing at 500 FPM. At sea level, the same rate may require burning only every 30 to 40 seconds. Burn rates cannot be predicted in advance, but practice will get you in the ballpark to begin with, and experimentation will find the correct burn rate for a particular day's ambient temperature, altitude, and balloon weight.

Another skill to develop in ascents is knowing when to quit burning so the balloon will slow and stop at the chosen altitude. The transition from a climbing mode to level flight involves estimating the momentum and coasting up to the desired or assigned altitude.

An ascent of 200 to 300 FPM is slow enough to detect wind changes at different altitudes, which is helpful in maneuvering. Above 500 FPM, it is possible to fly right through small, narrow wind bands, or a wind that its direction change is very small, without noticing. It is a good idea to launch and climb at a slow speed (100 to 200 FPM) to make an early decision which direction to fly.

If you practice and remember the routine, your flying skills will get better and better; it will be easier and easier to fly, and you will have more fun.

Descents

To start a descent from level flight, skip one burn, and then go back to the level-flight regimen to hold the descent at a constant rate.

To check winds below, look for the calm side of a pond, ripples on water, a flag, smoke, or movement of tall grass. You could also drop some tissue rolled into a small ball. The procedure for detecting wind speed and direction in a descent is similar to that of an ascent; a slow descent of 100 to 200 FPM allows you to make certain subtle changes.

A rapid descent in a balloon is a relative term, and is not defined. A 700 FPM descent started at 3,000 feet AGL is not necessarily rapid. A 700 FPM descent started at 300 feet AGL is rapid and may be critical. Rapid descents should be made with adequate ground clearance and distance from obstacles.

You can learn the classic balloon flare by matching the VSI to the altimeter, i.e., descend 500 FPM from 500 feet AGL, 400 FPM from 400 feet AGL, etc. Below 200 feet do not use instruments; look below for obstacles, especially powerlines.

Hot air balloons are equipped with a vent (which may be called *maneuvering vent* or *valve*). When opened, the vent releases hot air from the envelope and draws cooler air in at the mouth, thus reducing the overall temperature, allowing the balloon to descend.

Learn to calibrate the use of the vent, as well as the burners. Know how much air is being released so as to know what effect to expect. For predictability, time the vent openings, and open the vent precisely. Parachute vent balloons usually have a manufacturer's limitation on how long the vent may be open. Side vents may be used more liberally because the air being exhausted from the envelope is much cooler than air vented from a parachute top. A side vent opening of 5 seconds may be the equivalent of only 1 second of top vent. Use the vent sparingly; it should not be used instead of patience. Avoid using the vent to descend; use of the vent is wasteful and disruptive.

The only direct control of the balloon the pilot has is vertical motion. You can make the balloon go up by adding heat. You can make it come down by venting or not adding heat. For horizontal or lateral motion, you must rely on wind, which may or may not be going in the direction you wish to go. A good pilot learns to control vertical motion precisely and variably to provide maximum lateral choice.

MANEUVERING

The art of controlling the horizontal direction of a free balloon is the highest demonstration of ballooning skill. The balloon is officially a non-steerable aircraft. Despite the fact that balloons are non-dirigible, some pilots seem to be able to steer their balloons better than others.

There are broad physical laws that should be understood to help maneuver a balloon horizontally. For example, cold air flows downhill, hot air flows uphill, and in the Northern Hemisphere, as altitude is gained, wind is deflected to the right, or clockwise due to Coriolis force.

Being knowledgeable of the wind at various altitudes, both before launch and during flight, is the key factor for maneuvering. The following describes some ways you can determine wind conditions.

WINDS ABOVE

Pibal

Pibal is short for pilot balloon. Many balloon pilots believe that pibals are a must for determining local wind conditions. To deploy your own pibals, all you need is a bottle of helium and a bag of toy balloons.

A 9-inch, dark-colored toy balloon filled with helium will climb at a faster rate than a normal balloon climb-out and can be visible for over 1,000 feet AGL, even before official sunrise.

One method is to send up two or three pibals at 10 to 15 second intervals to fly at different altitudes. You can get them to climb at different rates and fly at different altitudes by diluting the helium with air. To do this, fill the balloon partially with helium and add some air by blowing with the mouth.

A 9-inch toy balloon filled to 7 inches with helium and topped off to 9 inches with a good puff of breath may show winds at different altitudes. The second balloon released will confirm the changes in direction made by the first balloon or show a completely different flightpath confirming variable or changing winds.

Other Balloons

Watch what other hot air balloons are doing, both before launch and while in the air. They make excellent pibals.

Winds Aloft Forecasts

Winds aloft forecasts are based on information gathered from weather balloons launched twice daily from widely scattered locations around the United States. This information is then transmitted to a central computer for processing into three different forecast periods for use during specific times.

As a result, when you call a Automated Flight Service Station (AFSS) for winds aloft, the forecast you receive will be based on information that may be several hours old. Also, you should be aware that no winds are forecast within 1,500 feet of station elevation. If the field elevation is 1,400 feet, the first level of winds forecast will be at 3,000 feet (1,600 feet AGL). If the field elevation is 4,600 feet, the first level of winds forecast will be at 9,000 feet (4,400 feet AGL).

If you are launching from a site other than near specific sites used in the forecasts, you may get an extrapolation of winds from several sites. Remember that the AFSS briefer is probably located at a site other than where the winds aloft are gathered. When calling the AFSS for the winds aloft for a launch, the briefer may give you an extrapolation of winds recorded at sites 50 to 100 miles away from your launch site. Also, the briefer may not tell you that the winds were an extrapolation. You should ask for the closest reporting sites and then make the extrapolation yourself.

In summary, remember winds aloft is a forecast, made by a machine, several hours old, and delivered to you by a person who may not be familiar enough with the geography of the area to select correct weather-reporting points for your use.
Winds aloft are best used only as raw data. You should get the winds aloft, record the forecast, compare it to the actual winds, and use the winds aloft forecast as a guide to make your own forecast.

Even if you have no aids to assist you, remember that winds can flow in different directions at different altitudes. As you ascend, pay attention to wind direction and how it changes. If you want to go in a certain direction, and a wind is available to take you there, fly at the altitude where that wind exists. Perhaps you cannot go directly to your selected location, but can reach it by flying in a zigzag pattern using different altitude winds alternately.

WINDS BELOW

When in flight, winds below can be observed in many ways. Observe smoke, trees, dust, flags, and especially ponds and lakes to see what the wind is doing on the ground. To make certain what is going on between your balloon and the ground, watch other balloons, if there are any.

Another means of checking winds below is to drop a very light object and watch it descend to the ground. However, exercise caution with this method. 14 CFR part 91 allows things to be dropped from the air that will not harm anything below. 14 CFR section 91.15: Dropping Objects, states "No pilot in command of a civil aircraft may allow any object to be dropped from that aircraft in flight that creates a hazard to persons or property. However, this section does not prohibit the dropping of any object if reasonable precautions are taken to avoid injury or damage to persons or property."

Some items that you may drop without creating a hazard are small, air-filled toy balloons, small balls made of a single piece of tissue, or a small glob of shaving cream from an aerosol can. A facial tissue, about 8″ x 8″, rolled into a sphere about the size of a ping-pong ball works well. These balls will fall at about 350 FPM, and can be seen for several hundred feet, and are convenient to carry. Counting as the tissue ball descends, you can estimate the heights of wind changes by comparing times to the ground with your altimeter. Experiment by dropping some of these objects, practice reading the indications, and plan accordingly.

CONTOUR FLYING

Contour flying may be the most fun and most challenging, but, at the same time, it may also be the most hazardous and most misunderstood of all balloon flight maneuvers. [Figure 4-1]

FIGURE 4-1.—Contour flying.

A good definition of contour flying is flying safely at low altitude, while obeying all regulations, considering persons, animals, and property on the ground. Safe contour flying means never creating a hazard to persons in the basket or on the ground, or to any property, including the balloon.

At first glance, the definition is subjective. One person's hazard may be another person's fun. For instance, a person who has never seen a balloon before may think a basket touching the surface of a lake is dangerous, while the pilot may believe a splash-and-dash is fun.

Regulations

Legal contour flying has a precise definition. While the FAA has not specifically defined contour, it has specified exactly what minimum altitudes are. 14 CFR part 91, section 91.119, refers to three different areas: anywhere, over congested areas, and over other than congested areas, including open water and sparsely populated areas.

More balloonists are issued FAA violations for low flying than for any other reason. Many pilots do not understand the minimum safe altitude regulation. A high percentage of balloonists believe the regulation was written for heavier-than-air aircraft and that it does not apply to balloons. The fact is, the regulation was written to protect persons and property on the ground and it applies to all aircraft, including balloons.

Since this regulation is so important to balloonists, the following is the printed applicable portion.

14 CFR part 91, section 91.119—Minimum safe altitudes: General (in part).

"Except when necessary for takeoff or landing, no person may operate an aircraft below the following altitudes:

(a) *Anywhere.* An altitude allowing, if a power unit fails, an emergency landing without undue hazard to persons or property on the surface.

(b) *Over congested areas.* Over any congested area of a city, town, or settlement, or over any open air assembly of persons, an altitude of 1,000 feet above the highest obstacle within a horizontal radius of 2,000 feet of the aircraft.

(c) *Over other than congested areas.* An altitude of 500 feet above the surface, except over open water or sparsely populated areas. In those cases, the aircraft may not be operated closer than 500 feet to any person, vessel, vehicle, or structure."

The regulation refers to aircraft. Balloons are aircraft; therefore, the regulation applies to balloons.

14 CFR part 91, section 91.119(a) requires a pilot to fly at an altitude that will allow for a power unit failure and/or an emergency landing without undo hazards to persons or property. All aircraft should be operated so as to be safe, even in worst-case conditions. Every good pilot is always thinking "what if...," and should operate accordingly.

This portion of the regulation can be applied in the following way. When climbing over an obstacle, you can make the balloon just clear the obstacle, fly over it with room to spare, or give the obstacle sufficient clearance to account for a problem, or miscalculation. An obstacle can be overflown while climbing, descending, or in level flight. You would have the most opportunity to misjudge the obstacle when in descending flight. In level flight the danger is reduced. You encounter the least hazard by climbing. Some instructors teach minimizing the hazard by climbing as you approach, thus giving room to coast over the obstacle in case of a burner malfunction.

14 CFR part 91, section 91.119(b) concerns flying over congested areas, such as settlements, towns, cities, and gatherings of people. You must stay 1,000 feet above the highest obstacle within a 2,000-foot radius of the balloon. This is a straightforward regulation and easy to understand. Note that the highest obstacle will probably be a transmitting antenna, or some tall object, not the rooftops. Two thousand feet is almost half a mile.

A good pilot should add chicken farms, turkey farms, and dairies to the 1,000-feet-above rule. Domestic animals, while not specifically mentioned in the regulations, are considered to be property, and experienced pilots know that chickens, ducks, turkeys, swine, horses, and cows are sometimes spooked by the overflight of a balloon. Livestock in large fields seem to be less bothered by balloons; however, it is always a good idea to stay at least 700 feet away from domestic animals.

14 CFR part 91, section 91.119(c) has two parts: sparsely populated and unpopulated. Here the pilot must stay at least 500 feet away from persons, vehicles, vessels, and structures. Away from is the secret to understanding this rule. The regulation specifies how high above the ground the pilot must be and also states the pilot may never operate closer than 500 feet.

There exists a possibility for misunderstanding in interpreting the difference between congested and other than congested. Where does congested area end and other than congested area begin. For example, operating below 1,000 feet AGL within 2,000 feet of a congested area is in violation of 14 CFR part 91, section 91.119(b), even though the bordering area may be used only for agricultural purposes. Therefore, if you are flying over unpopulated land near a housing tract, you must fly either above 1,000 feet AGL, or stay 2,000 feet away from the houses.

14 CFR part 91, section 91.119 is a very important regulation and is often misunderstood. In coastal areas, pilots often receive violations from the FAA for flying low along or near people on otherwise deserted beaches. The pilot will say, "But I was not over the people, I was 100 yards out over the water." The regulation states 500 feet away from, not 500 feet over. There is a definite difference.

To stay 500 feet away from an isolated farmhouse, for instance, imagine a 1,000-foot diameter clear hemisphere centered over the building. If you are 400 feet away from the structure on the horizontal plane, you only need to fly about 300 feet AGL to be 500 feet away from it. If the balloon passes directly over the building, then you must be a minimum of 500 feet above the rooftop, chimney, or television antenna to be legal.

In summary, regulations require: (1) flying high enough to be safe if you have a problem; (2) 1,000 feet above the highest obstacle within a 2,000-foot radius above a congested area; and (3) an altitude of 500 feet above the surface, except over open water or sparsely populated areas. In those cases, the balloon may not be operated closer than 500 feet to any person, vessel, vehicle, or structure. This is an easy-to-understand regulation, and must be complied with. The minimum altitude regulations are those most often broken by balloonists. If you understand the regulation, you should have no problem complying with it.

The balloon practical test standard (PTS) asks the applicant to demonstrate contour flying by using all flight controls properly, to maintain the desired altitude based on the appropriate clearance over terrain and obstacles, consistent with safety. The pilot must consider the effects of wind gusts, wind shear, thermal activity and orographic conditions, and allow adequate clearance for livestock and other animals.

Contour Flying Techniques

Aside from the legal aspects, contour flying is probably the most difficult flying to perform. Since most contour flying is done in unpopulated areas, the balloon is rarely higher than 500 feet AGL, and therefore the balloon's flight instruments are seldom observed. Because mechanical instruments have several seconds lag, and electronic instruments are very sensitive, pilots must rely on their observation and judgment. Regardless of the type of instruments in the balloon basket, the human eye is by far the best gauge when operating close to the ground.

When flying at low altitude, the pilot must be vigilant for obstacles, especially powerlines and traffic, and not rely solely on instruments inside the basket. The pilot should always face the direction of travel, especially at low altitude. The pilot's feet, hips, and shoulders should be facing forward. The pilot should turn only his or her head from side to side (not the entire body) to gauge altitude and to detect or confirm climbs and descents. Facing forward cannot be overemphasized. There are many National Transportation Safety Board (NTSB) and FAA accident reports describing balloon contacts with ground obstacles because the pilot was looking in another direction.

Contour flying may require shorter burns than the standard burn. To fly at low altitudes requires half or quarter burns. One disadvantage in using small pops is you can lose track of the heat you are making and become very noisy. Precise altitude control requires special burner technique. Another hazard of a series of too-small burns is that added heat becomes cumulative and you add heat before you have evaluated the effects of the last burn. The balloon actually responds to a burn 10 to 20 seconds after the burner is used. The choo-choo method of blast valve use adds heat before you know the effect of previous burns, is an annoying sound, and makes the pilot appear undecided.

Contour flying is a complex operation. You must see all obstacles on or near the balloon path, and remember their location. You must estimate the terrain or obstacle height, and always be prepared for an unexpected situation. You must establish a relationship between the balloon attitude and the terrain or obstacle height. An estimate must be made of the delay between the time you command the balloon to perform and the time you want the balloon to fly the selected flight profile. Be prepared to adjust your estimates. All these mental calculations must occur in a few seconds, over and over again, as you fly a complicated flight profile.

One technique to determine if the balloon is ascending, flying level, or descending is to compare two not-too-distant objects at the side of the balloon path. If you look directly ahead, or forward and down, objects on the ground are getting larger as you approach them and you tend to think you are descending. Just the opposite may occur if you look at the ground to the rear of the balloon. As you see objects getting smaller as they move away from you, you may think you are climbing. While you want to maintain vigilance looking ahead in the direction of flight, you must still scan as much as 45° to either side and avoid the possible distortion of looking straight ahead.

What you look for is two objects some distance from the balloon and some distance from each other in a straight line. By comparing the relative movement, you can tell if the balloon is ascending or descending. If the nearer object seems to be getting taller in relation to the far object, you are descending. Conversely, if the farther object seems to be getting taller when compared to the near object, you are ascending.

Some favorite sighting objects are a power pole as the near object and the line of a road, field, or orchard as the far object, because you can observe the line moving up or down the pole. Water towers with checkerboard or striped markings are also good sighting objects. Remember that vigilance is required to constantly scan the terrain along your path, and you must be alert to avoid becoming fixated on your sighting objects. Look where you are flying.

Some Disadvantages and Bad Practices

The line between contour flying and unsafe, inconsiderate, and misunderstood practices can sometimes be very fine.

Aborted Landings

People often misinterpret aborted landings on the ground as buzzing or rude flying. Sometimes landing sites seem to be elusive. A typical situation has the pilot descending to land at an appropriate site, but the pilot has miscalculated the winds below and the balloon turns away from the open field toward a farmhouse. "Oops, got to go back up and look for another landing site," thinks the pilot. What is the farmer on the ground thinking? The farmer sees the balloon descend, turn towards the house, and then, with noisy burners roaring, zoom back into the air and proceed. A perfect case of buzzing. The pilot was not being rude or evil, just inconsiderate, inexperienced, or both. The pilot did not mean to swoop down to buzz the house; the wind changed.

Had the pilot watched something drop from the basket to gauge the winds below, or been more observant, the pilot would have known the balloon would turn towards the house as it descended. A squirt of shaving foam from an aerosol can, or a small piece of rolled up tissue could have told the pilot of the wind change at lower altitudes.

Two or three of these swoops over a sparsely populated area, and people on the ground may not only think the pilot is buzzing houses, some people may think the pilot is having a problem and is in trouble. That is when the well-meaning landowner calls the police to report a "balloon in trouble."

Flying too close to a house (your friend's house, for example) to say hello, dragging the field, giving people a thrill by flying too low over a gathering, are examples of buzzing, which is illegal and can be hazardous.

Identification of Animal Population

Balloonists must learn how to locate and identify animals on the ground. Even though it may be legal to fly at a certain low altitude, animals do not know the laws, nor do most of their owners. If you cause dogs to bark, turkeys to panic, or horses to run, even while flying legally, you may provide legitimate cause for complaint.

Flight Direction

Balloon direction change usually comes with altitude change. Balloon pilots ascend and descend looking for different winds, a procedure most people on the ground do not understand. A good citizen, meaning to be helpful, may call the police or fire department, thinking a balloonist is in trouble; many authorities assume calls are only from upset or threatened people.

Some disadvantages of low flying are: the noise may frighten animals and children; the balloon's shadow may spook livestock; people may think the balloonist is in trouble; the balloon may hit tall obstacles; the pilot has less time to correct or adjust for a mechanical problem; the pilot is more likely to be distracted when flying low, when a distraction can be most hazardous.

The particular pleasures of contour flying can best be enjoyed in a balloon. It is wonderful to fly at low level over the trees, drop down behind the orchard; float across the pond just off the water; watch jackrabbits scatter; and see sights close up. No other aircraft can perform low-level contour flying, as safely as a balloon and in no other aircraft is the flight as beautiful.

Contour flying can be great fun, but remember that the balloon should always be flown at legal, safe, and considerate altitudes.

RADIO COMMUNICATIONS

All balloon pilots should have basic knowledge of correct radio procedures as airspace is getting more complicated, and aviation radios are required in many areas. Balloon instructors should be teaching aviation radio procedures to students because it is specifically required during practical tests.

Aviation radios (VHF) may be used for communications between pilot and control tower, pilot and AFSS, air-to-air (pilot-to-pilot), or air-to-ground (pilot-to-crew), and to get information from Automatic Terminal Information Service (ATIS) and Automatic Weather Observing System (AWOS). Only specific frequencies may be used for each type of communication. [Figure 4-2]

FIGURE 4-2.—Radio equipment.

Clarity and Brevity

The single, most important aspect of radio communications is clarity. Brevity is also important, and contacts should be kept as brief as possible. All frequencies are shared with others.

Procedural Words and Phrases

The Pilot/Controller Glossary found in the Aeronautical Information Manual (AIM), published periodically by the FAA, contains correct language for communication between a pilot and Air Traffic Control (ATC). Good phraseology enhances safety and is the mark of a professional pilot. Following are some common words and phrases from the AIM.

- "**ABEAM**—An aircraft is abeam a fix, point, or object when that fix, point, or object is approximately 90 degrees to the right or left of the aircraft track. Abeam indicates a general position rather than a precise point."
- "**ACKNOWLEDGE**—Let me know that you have received my message."
- "**AFFIRMATIVE**—Yes."
- "**CLEARED FOR TAKEOFF**—ATC authorization for an aircraft to depart. It is predicted on known traffic and known physical airport conditions."
- "**CLEARED TO LAND**—ATC authorization for an aircraft to land. It is predicted on known traffic and known physical airport conditions."
- "**EXPEDITE**—Used by ATC when prompt compliance is required to avoid the development of an imminent situation."
- "**FIX**—A geographical position determined by visual reference to the surface, by reference to one or more radio NAVAIDs, by celestial plotting, or by another navigational device" (such as GPS).
- "**GO AHEAD**—Proceed with your message. Not to be used for any other purpose."
- "**HAVE NUMBERS**—Used by pilots to inform ATC that they have received runway, wind, and altimeter information only."
- "**HOW DO YOU HEAR ME?**—A question relating to the quality of the transmission or to determine how well the transmission is being received."
- "**IMMEDIATELY**—Used by ATC when such action compliance is required to avoid an imminent situation."
- "**I SAY AGAIN**—The message will be repeated."
- "**LOCAL TRAFFIC**—Aircraft operating in the traffic pattern or within sight of the tower, or aircraft known to be departing or arriving from flight in local practice areas, or aircraft executing practice instrument approaches at the airport."
- "**MAYDAY**—The international radiotelephony distress signal. When repeated three times, it indicates imminent and grave danger and that immediate assistance is requested."
- "**MINIMUM FUEL**—Indicates that an aircraft's fuel supply has reached a stage where, upon reaching the destination, it can accept little or no delay. This is not an emergency situation but merely indicates an emergency situation is possible should any undue delay occur."
- "**NEGATIVE**—'No,' or 'permission not granted,' or 'that is not correct.'"
- "**OUT**—The conversation is ended and no response is expected."
- "**OVER**—My transmission is ended and no response is expected."
- "**PAN-PAN**—The international radiotelephony urgency signal. When repeated three times, indicates uncertainty or alert followed by the nature of the urgency."
- "**PILOT'S DISCRETION**—When used in conjunction with altitude assignments, means that ATC has offered the pilot the option of starting climb or descent whenever he wishes and conducting the climb or descent at any rate he wishes. He may temporarily level off at any intermediate attitude. However, once

he has vacated an attitude, he may not return to that attitude."

- "**RADIO**—(a) A device used for communication. (b) Used to refer to a flight service station; e.g., 'Seattle Radio' is used to call Seattle FSS."
- "**READ BACK**—Repeat my message back to me."
- "**REPORT**—Used to instruct pilots to advise ATC of specified information; e.g., 'Report passing Hamilton VOR.'"
- "**ROGER**—I have received all of your last transmission. It should not be used to answer a question requiring a yes or no answer."
- "**SAY AGAIN**—Used to request a repeat of the last transmission. Usually specifies transmission or portion thereof not understood or received; e.g., 'Say again all after ABRAM VOR.'"
- "**SAY ALTITUDE**—Used by ATC to ascertain an aircraft's specific altitude/flight level. When the aircraft is climbing or descending, the pilot should state the indicated altitude rounded to the nearest 100 feet."
- "**SAY HEADING**—Used by ATC to request an aircraft heading. The pilot should state the actual heading of the aircraft."
- "**SPEAK SLOWER**—Used in verbal communications as a request to reduce speech rate."
- "**THAT IS CORRECT**—The understanding you have is right."
- "**UNABLE**—Indicates inability to comply with a specific instruction, request, or clearance."
- "**URGENCY**—A condition of being concerned about safety and of requiring timely but not immediate assistance; a potential distress condition."
- "**VERIFY**—Request confirmation of information; e.g., 'verify assigned altitude.'"
- "**WILCO**—I have received your message, understand it, and will comply with it."

Jargon, chatter, and CB slang have no place in ATC communications.

Radio Technique

Listen before you transmit. Many times you can get the information you want through ATIS, or by listening to other conversations on the frequency. Do not clutter the airwaves with irrelevant information. Wait for an obvious break in broadcasts. Do not interrupt. Think before keying your transmitter. Know what you want to say. If it is lengthy, jot it down first.

The microphone should be very close to your lips. After pressing the mike button, a slight pause may be necessary to be sure the first word is transmitted. Speak in a normal conversational tone.

Remember to release the mike button after you speak or you will be unable to receive.

Contact Procedures

The term initial contact or initial call-up means the first radio call you make to a given facility, or the first call to a different controller/AFSS specialist within a facility.

Use the following format: (1) name of facility being called, (2) your full aircraft identification (the prefix "November" for "N" is omitted), (3) the type of message to follow or your request if it is short, and (4) the word over if required.

Examples:

LIVERMORE TOWER, BALLOON FOUR THREE ONE AT THE BALLOON FIELD READY TO LAUNCH WITH BRAVO (The ID of ATIS message "B".)

LIVERMORE TOWER, BALLOON FIVE FIVE SIX THREE WHISKEY, WITH YOU AT TWO THOUSAND FEET OVER THE CITY, EASTBOUND.

For subsequent contacts and responses to call-up from a ground facility, use the same format as used for initial contact except state your message or request with the call-up in one transmission. The ground station and the word over may be omitted if the message requires an obvious reply and there is no possibility for misunderstanding.

Aircraft Call Signs

Generally, the prefix N is dropped and the aircraft manufacturer's name or model is stated instead. In the case of balloons, the word *balloon* should precede the registration number.

Examples:
BALLOON SIX FIVE FIVE GOLF

BALLOON FIVE ONE FOUR SEVEN NINER

Using the word *balloon* is recommended because ATC may not be familiar with balloon makes and models. If the controller does not respond appropriately, precede your registration number with "hot air balloon." Some balloon makes could be confused with certain airplane makes.

Time

The FAA uses Coordinated Universal Time (UTC)—also known as Greenwich Mean Time (GMT) or Zulu Time (Z)—for all operations.

The 24-hour clock system is used in radiotelephone transmissions. The first two figures and the minutes indicate the hour by the last two figures.

***Examples*:**
0000: ZERO ZERO ZERO ZERO (12 o'clock midnight)

0920: ZERO NINER TWO ZERO (9:20 a.m.)

Figures

Figures indicating hundreds and thousands in round numbers, as for ceiling heights and upper wind levels up to 9,900 are spoken in accordance with the following examples:

500: FIVE HUNDRED
4500: FOUR THOUSAND FIVE HUNDRED (Not forty-five hundred)

Numbers above 9,900 are spoken by separating the digits preceding the word "thousand" as follows:

10000: ONE ZERO THOUSAND (10,000)

13500: ONE THREE THOUSAND FIVE HUNDRED (13,500)

Altitudes

Altitudes up to but not including 18,000 feet MSL are spoken by stating the separate digits of the thousands, plus the hundreds, if appropriate, and rounded. They are always MSL.

Examples:
450: FOUR HUNDRED FIFTY

1,200: ONE THOUSAND TWO HUNDRED (Not twelve hundred)

12,500: ONE TWO THOUSAND FIVE HUNDRED (Not twelve thousand five hundred)

Phonetic Alphabet

Pilots should use the correct phonetic alphabet when identifying their aircraft during initial contact with ATC facilities. Additionally, use the phonetic equivalents for single letters and to spell out groups of letters or difficult words during difficult communications conditions.

A good way to learn radio language is to visit a tower, or sit in the parking lot with a receiver, and listen to the conversations.

Uses of a VHF Radio

There is confusion among pilots as to which frequencies may be used from air-to-ground, balloon-to-chase crew, for instance. Many balloonists use 123.3 and 123.5 for air-to-ground (pilot-to-chase crew), as these frequencies are for glider schools and not many soaring planes are in the air at sunrise. Since all users of the airwaves must have an ID or call, ground crews identify themselves by adding chase to the aircraft call sign. For example, the chase call for "Balloon 12345" would be "12345 Chase."

Air-to-air is 122.75. Remember that everyone in the air is using this frequency, so keep your transmissions brief. A balloon pilot trying to contact a circling airplane would try 122.75 first. Weather information is available on VHF radio. A balloon pilot could obtain nearby weather reports by tuning to the ATIS. [Refer to appendix A] The appropriate frequency is listed on the cover of the sectional chart, and in the airport information block printed on the chart near the appropriate airport.

Another source of weather information is the AWOS. AWOS frequencies may be found in the Airport/ Facility Directory published by the National Ocean Service (NOAA) and available at the local pilots supply store or by subscription.

If you want to actually speak with a weather briefer, you can call the nearest AFSS on any of several frequencies. Flight Watch, the en route flight advisory service that provides timely weather information upon pilot request, can be reached on 122.0.

CHAPTER 5

POSTFLIGHT PROCEDURES

This chapter discusses postflight procedures. Included are deflation, pack-up and recovery, and propane management and fueling.

DEFLATION

There is much more to deflating a hot air balloon than just letting the air out of the envelope. A picture-book deflation is one in which the pilot guides the balloon to the selected landing site containing no obstacles, pulls the deflation line and lays the balloon down perfectly, ready to be packed up.

Wind Conditions

Different wind conditions require different deflation procedures. A light wind allows several options. For example, the balloon while still inflated may be moved, or walked from the landing site, to a better deflation site. This should be done very carefully, with the pilot in command in the basket, in charge of the entire operation, and assistants on the ground. Walking the balloon on the ground should be done with the understanding that the wind may increase at any time and that the pilot and crew should be prepared to deal with the wind. The pilot and crew should have a brief discussion to plan the movement and alternatives if the wind comes up. The pilot should get the balloon light, so the crew does not have to lift the balloon, but merely move it sideways. This maneuver can be accomplished if the wind is calm or nearly calm, and the balloon can be moved only at a slight angle to the wind. The balloon must be moved very slowly as the average balloon has the momentum of a couple of tons. No crewmember should be directly in front of the balloon and the pilot should control the altitude with tiny, evenly-spaced burns to hold equilibrium at about 1 to 3 feet above ground level. Everyone in the crew should know in advance the intended stopping place so they can work together.

In light winds, the crew has time to inspect the proposed deflation site and remove small sticks and sharp objects that could puncture the envelope. Check bushes and weeds for anything unfriendly to the envelope. Some balloonists use a huge tarp to cover the ground and protect the envelope.

Once the site is selected, the deflation should proceed. If the balloon is equipped with a pyrometer wire, disconnect it and stow it out of the way. On most systems the deflation line must be tended and held with constant tension to keep the deflation port open.

No-wind Deflation

Deflation in no-wind situations can have some problems. Since you do not want the envelope to fall straight down and gift-wrap the heater/basket assembly, most pilots ask a crewmember to use the crown line to pull the envelope away from the basket. Unless properly instructed, the person on the top line will usually pull the envelope completely over until the deflation port is no longer at the top, and the envelope will not deflate. Oftentimes, in this situation, you or a crewmember must tackle the envelope bodily and wrestle the hot air out. This can be hard on the envelope and the crewmember.

A standup deflation with no wind should not be a lot of work. First, turn off the fuel at all tanks, open the blast valves, burn off any fuel remaining in the lines, and turn off pilot lights. Then, the top is opened and held open while you waits, watching the suspension lines. When the suspension lines start to sag and go limp, the basket should be tipped over toward the desired direction of deflation. The envelope is then gently pulled down, starting at the underside of the mouth and stopping at the equator. This allows the top of the envelope to stay on top and the hot air inside the envelope to escape naturally. The envelope is handled much less, crew expends less energy, and the envelope lies gently down.

Light-wind Deflation

The light-wind deflation is the easiest of all. In a wind of 2 to 5 knots, the pilot need only pull the deflation line, tip the basket over, and watch the envelope slowly lay itself on the ground. The deflation port will stay on top most of the time and the crew holds the port open only at the very end of the deflation to let the last of the air out.

High-wind Deflation

High-wind deflations become a part of the landing. As the balloon approaches the ground, you should prepare to activate the deflation vent at the appropriate time and the wind will do the rest. The next thing you know, the balloon is on its side, and the air is all out of the envelope. Some manufacturers have restrictions regarding activating the deflation port above ground, so you must be familiar with manufacturer instructions.

PREPARING FOR PACK-UP

The last element of the deflation is getting the envelope ready to be packed into its bag. Before all the air is out of the envelope, and while you can still look into the deflation port and see the deflation panel and control line, pull the panel back into place near the port, and some of the control line back up into the top part of the envelope.

If the balloon has a parachute top, placing the deflation panel in its correct position at deflation requires less handling of the envelope fabric. This makes preparing the top for the next launch much easier.
Hook-and-look fastened on panels should be reinstalled after deflation. There are several good reasons for putting the top in at the landing site rather than waiting until the next launch. By mating the fastener right away, you prevent contamination from sticks, leaves, and dirt. If you inflate next from wet grass, the fastener will already be sealed and will not become contaminated with moisture. Hook-and-loop fasteners mated wet have less strength than fasteners mated dry, even if subsequent wetting occurs. Hook-and-loop fasteners mate stronger with pressure and motion. While the envelope is in its bag, with the top of the envelope at the bottom of the bag, there are 200 pounds of fabric squeezing the fastener together while the motion of the chase vehicle vibrates the fastener into a strong connection.

After pulling the top open, there is usually a pile of control line(s) at the bottom of the envelope or in the basket. Tie off each control line separately at the mouth of the envelope to eliminate tangles during pack-up. Some balloons have as many as four control lines (deflation, vent, and two rotators) hanging out of the mouth.

Another operation that saves time at the next launch is to pull some of the deflation line back up to the top of the envelope so that, if the line is inadvertently pulled during layout, the top will not be pulled out of place.

Always remove direct-reading pyrometers from the envelope before completing deflation to prevent damage to the fabric or instrument. Electric and remote-reading pyrometer wires should be disconnected from their gauge in the basket to prevent wire breakage and connector damage. Remote-reading pyrometers using a transmitter/sensor do not have the long wire to contend with, but the transmitter and the fabric around it may need some protection. Envelopes with control-line pulleys are subject to damage by fabric becoming jammed into the pulley. During deflation, the lines should be pulled clear to the top of the envelope to prevent damage during pack-up and layout. Envelopes with steel cable control lines require extra care as sliding the cable through a tightly bunched bundle of fabric causes additional damage to the fabric.

Carefully squeeze the air out of the envelope prior to packing it in its bag to avoid unnecessary handling. The air should be evacuated through the deflation panel or mouth and not through the fabric. A nonporous envelope allows air to escape only through needle holes in the seams. If pressure is applied, enlargement of the holes may occur.

Careful deflation and preparing the envelope properly helps to provide a positive beginning for the next flight.

It would be nice to have biodegradable balloons that could just be left in the field to dissolve and disappear in the morning dew, to fertilize the soil! Then you would not have to figure out how to get the balloon back in the van or pickup, or back onto the trailer. You would avoid the hardest part of ballooning, the recovery and pack-up.

Recovery

Ease of recovery should never take precedence over getting the balloon down without harm to passengers or people and property on the ground, damage to the balloon, or disruption to the environment. Recovery is really a chase crew term, because the pilot has always had possession of the balloon. It is the ground crew that had the balloon fly away and now wants to recover it. For some, perhaps the perfect recovery is when the balloon makes a return flight and lands at the launch site, allowing the crew to wait for it to come back.

Most pilots consider the perfect landing site one that allows an easy recovery. However, as pointed out in the chapter on landings, recovery is one of the least important elements of the landing.

The easiest recovery is when the balloon can be reached by public roads and goes directly from the landing site into the chase vehicle without unusual conversation, dismantling, carrying, or packing. If there is no wind, the balloon may be moved to the chase vehicle while it is still inflated. Just be sure to stay clear of powerlines.

Recovery from difficult terrain (no roads) or a difficult landing site (a tree, for example) are problems that are best dealt with by a strong and enthusiastic crew. Some planning can alleviate problems with recovery from difficult places.

If you have to carry the balloon a long distance, the first step in the recovery process is to break down the balloon into small pieces. Carrying many separate components (basket, heater system, and envelope, for instance) may be much easier than trying to move the entire balloon in only one or two pieces. If your crew is very small, one pilot and one passenger, for example, move the envelope in its bag by rolling it like a giant snowball. The basket may be slid on its own skids rather than being lifted completely off the ground. With a four-member crew, any AX8 or smaller balloon can be moved by having one person on the corner of each major component.

Recovery from snow requires some special equipment. How do you carry an envelope when you are waist deep in snow? A toboggan or large garbage can lid can be a good cargo sled.

Be creative and do not cause harm. If you are flying at an event and land in a difficult location, do not be embarrassed to ask other pilots and crews to help. Most balloonists are glad to help a fellow pilot.

Pack-up

Pack-up means getting the balloon into condition for transport and storage, and, in some ways, prepared for the next flight. Part of the pack-up procedure may be considered preflight preparations for the next flight.

The sooner the balloon is packed up, the better. Once you have determined that the passengers are cared for, you should, with the help of crew (and passengers, if appropriate), prepare the envelope and stuff it in its bag. The fabric will degrade lying in the sun.

Making sure the balloon is properly prepared for storage is important since you may not necessarily know when your next flight will be. (Particularly in winter, when inclement weather may prevent flying.) If, for example, the balloon gets wet, you must make sure you dry it thoroughly before packing it for storage, whether it is for a week or a month.

Check the temperature indicators, commonly called *tell-tales* located at the top of the envelope. If the temperature has exceeded manufacturer limitations, the fabric may require testing before the next flight. This is the first step in the preflight inspection for your next flight.

Determine that control lines are clear of fabric and fasten the ends at the mouth so they will not be lost inside the envelope, or tangled. By doing this, they will be readily available for layout the next flight.

If the deflation panel is sealed prior to stuffing the envelope into its bag, some time is saved at the launch site for the next flight. If the top hook-and-loop fastenings of the rip panel are mated at the landing site, dirt, debris, and water contamination are less likely to occur. In addition, the fastening becomes tightly mated while under the weight of the envelope during transportation. This saves unnecessary handling of the closure, which can result in premature fabric failure in that area. With a parachute top, even if the locating hook-and-pile tabs are not mated, the top of the balloon receives much less handling if the parachute is pulled into place during deflation or before pack-up.

If you pack your balloon the same way each time, you will not have to figure out how to orient the envelope in the predawn hours as you prepare for a flight. Packing your balloon and stowing it in the chase vehicle is the hardest work of a balloon flight, but remember that it is also part of preparing for your next flight.

PROPANE MANAGEMENT AND FUELING

The primary source of heat for a hot air balloon is propane. A pilot should be familiar with propane and the balloon's fuel system in order to properly manage fuel and refuel safely.

Properties of Propane

Propane is a colorless, odorless flammable gas (C_3H_8) found as a by-product of natural gas and the production of gasoline. Since pure propane has no smell; it is odorized with a warning agent.

Liquid petroleum gas (LPG) includes propane and butane. Propane is a gas at normal temperatures, but will liquefy under moderate pressure. It is usually stored in liquid form and is burned in vapor form. The potential fire hazard for propane is similar to that of natural gas, except that propane is heavier than air and will sink to the ground.

The boiling point of pure propane is -44°F. Since vaporization is quick at normal temperatures; propane does not present a flammable liquid hazard.

Propane is particularly suitable as fuel for hot air balloons because it is low in weight (4.2 pounds per gallon), high in thermal output, and its moderate tank pressure requires no pumps to deliver it to the balloon heater system. Propane is readily available at a reasonable price, clean, and safe.

Propane does have some disadvantages. Propane vapor is invisible, making it difficult to detect, and is heavier than air, which makes it pool or gather in low places. It is also very cold; giving freeze burns to skin if handled incorrectly.

Balloon Propane Tanks

Propane tanks used in hot air balloons are mainly constructed of either aluminum or stainless steel. Most aluminum tanks are vertical 10-gallon cylinders (DOT 4E240), built primarily for forklift trucks. Stainless steel tanks are either vertical or horizontal, of many different sizes, and built especially for hot air balloons. [Figure 5-1]

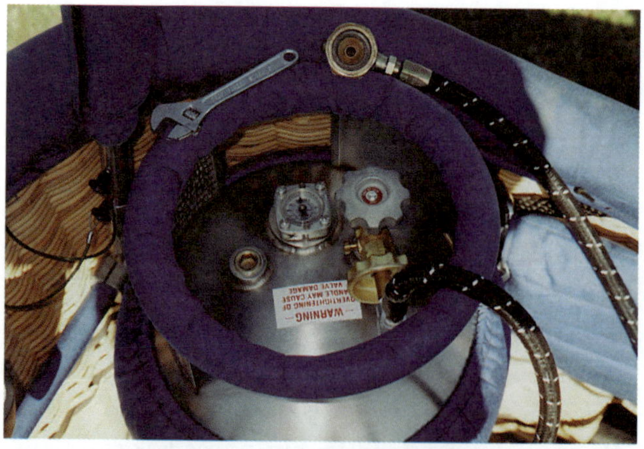

FIGURE 5-1.—Propane tank.

All balloon cylinders have liquid service valves, excess-pressure relief valves, and liquid level indicator valves. Many tanks have vapor service for pilot lights and some have an emergency valve or filler valve. Some tanks may have as many as five individual service valves, and some have only one combination (3-in-1) valve. There is no standard valve configuration for balloons. Generally, the large valve handle is liquid and the smaller handle is vapor; tanks and/or handles are usually labeled.

Propane Storage

Store propane tanks in a cool, ventilated place, away from ignition sources, flammable materials, and low places where a leak would form a pool of vapor. Do not store propane in a room or garage containing a water heater or furnace with a pilot light.

Always store propane tanks with the excess-pressure relief valve on top so that if the pressure should rise, the tank will vent vapor, not liquid.

Aluminum cylinders designed for either vertical or horizontal use have a special universal vent that should always be on top.

Selecting a Propane Company

All type-certificated hot air balloons in the United States use propane fuel. Supposedly there is only one grade of propane. The fact is, propane fuel purchased from a propane supplier may be a blend of propane and butane. Although butane is not readily available in its pure form, it is a by-product that is used during the summer months to reduce the tank pressure of propane.

Propane is used mostly as rural and industrial heating fuel. In the hot summer months, outdoor propane storage tanks, sitting in the sun, can develop high pressure, and propane suppliers may add butane to keep the pressure lowered. Balloonists sometimes have a problem in the fall or early winter when their propane supplier may be selling old stock, still containing a percentage of butane, which has low pressure when cold. To avoid low-pressure propane in the winter, purchase your balloon fuel from an operator who pumps large quantities of propane and has a fresh stock.

The price of propane varies widely and can be purchased from gas stations, recreational vehicle (RV) and trailer rental companies, trailer parks, campgrounds, and propane companies.

Balloonists in rural areas have the advantage of being able to have their own storage tanks and decanting fuel into their balloons. Propane distributors will rent storage tanks and fill them on a regular basis for a reasonable price. All you need to do is provide a legal place to put the tank, which usually involves clearance from buildings and property lines and a concrete slab or blocks to mount the tank. The propane company provides a tank of suitable size with a liquid feed hose and you can transfer liquid by differential pressure.

In some states there are discounts for using clean fuels (propane is very clean) and highway or motor vehicle taxes are deducted for use in certain vehicles. On the other hand, some states charge balloons aviation fuel taxes.

All balloonists, regardless of how they usually receive their propane, should know how to pump their own propane, and should own their own propane line adapters.

Fueling Safety

All fueling should be accomplished outside in the open air. Avoid fueling inside a van, bus, or closed trailer. Make sure there are not any sources of ignition nearby. Remove strikers and loose igniters from the basket. Because of static electricity, do not wear synthetic clothing in the fueling area. No one should smoke in the fueling area. Although a cigarette may not create sufficient heat to ignite propane, a cigarette lighter will. Do not allow spectators and nonessential persons to loiter nearby, and do not allow anyone in the balloon basket while tanks are being filled.

Everyone involved in fueling should wear gloves. Preferably, they should be smooth leather, loose fitting, and easy to remove. If a glove does get a blast of liquid propane, it will freeze, be very cold, and you will want to get the glove off fast.

Keep a large operable chemical fire extinguisher nearby and make sure everyone involved knows how to use it.

Fueling

Connect your adapter to the tank(s) to be filled, and connect the filler hose to the adapter. Check for leaks by opening a tank valve l/4-turn. Better to find the leak when it is small than after the main supply valve is open and/or the fuel pump is on.

If there are no leaks, open the tank valve full, then back 1/4-turn. Open the liquid level indicator valve (also called the 10 percent, 15 percent, 20 percent, or spit valve) 1/4-turn. There is no need to open the liquid level indicator valve any more than 1/4-turn if a pump is being used; it is only an indicator and the less it is opened, the easier and faster it will be to close. If fuel is going to be transferred by pressure differential (often called decanting), you should open the 10 percent valve to its full flow (about one complete turn) because you are trying to lower the pressure in the receiving tank so the propane will flow from high pressure (the filling tank) to low pressure (the receiving tank). Now the filler hose valve may be opened and the fuel pump turned on.

There are only two ways to determine legally when a propane tank is full, (1) from the liquid level indicator valve spitting, or (2) from the weight of the fuel. Even if the tank has a full-scale fuel gauge (0-100 percent), it is not a legal measure.

As soon as the indicator valve spits, close the supply valve and shut off the pump. Close the tank valve and then close the indicator valve. There is a common tendency to shut off the indicator valve first, but to avoid overfilling the tank, the supply valve should be closed first.

Be careful draining the hoses, even if the system has a bleed valve, as the propane drained from the filler hose is cold and may burn bare skin.

Disconnect all filler hoses, reconnect the balloon fuel lines, and check for leaks. Do not leave your hoses open for nesting insects or dirt, and do not wait until later to discover a leak. Put your system back together and check it now.

Never overfill propane tanks. Propane expands with heat and adequate head space must be allowed in the tank. When the spit valve spits, shut off the fuel supply.

Fueling Equipment

The hose coming off most propane suppliers' storage tanks does not fit into most balloon tank's liquid valve; therefore, an adapter is necessary. It is good practice to carry and use your own adapter, as most propane company adapters are worn and dirty and may damage your fuel system.

Prolonging Hose Life

Some people fuel through the balloon's fuel lines because it takes less time. This is not a good idea. Fittings from fuel lines to the burners are not designed to be used over and over. Fittings become rusted because the cadmium plating is worn off by wrenches. Fittings, possibly hoses, may then have to be replaced, depending upon their serviceability. If you insist on fueling through the lines, you should use two wrenches so you do not disturb the burner fitting.

Another reason to have special fueling hose adapters, and not to use the balloon fuel system, is that foreign matter (dirt, rust, pieces of rubber, etc.) may become lodged in your fuel hose. It is much better, and safer, if such matter lodges in an adapter, or falls to the bottom of the tank.

Hoses wear out by rubbing against things. When you are fueling, make sure the fuel hoses are not abraded in the process. During preventive maintenance, check the position and security of hoses.

Propane is an appropriate and safe fuel for hot air balloons, providing proper handling techniques and safety precautions are followed.

Fuel Management

Fuel systems are not standardized among manufacturers. Certificated balloons vary from a simple one-burner/one-tank system to complex systems with three burners and eight tanks. Some tanks are connected individually, some in series. Some systems have more tanks than hoses requiring the pilot to disconnect and connect hoses in flight. It is very easy to figure out a fuel management program for a one-burner, one-tank balloon, but what is the best fuel management system for a more complex system?

Most balloon fuel tank gauges are inaccurate. Vertical tanks do not have room for the fuel gauge float arm to read on a full-scale dial, and usually have dials that read from 5 to 35 percent. Horizontal tanks allow adequate room for the float arm and usually read from 0 to 100 percent. Tank gauge floats often stick and do not move.

Through experience and good record keeping, a pilot can develop the expertise to know approximately how much fuel is required per hour. A wristwatch can be a very dependable fuel gauge.

The best way to learn the fuel consumption of a balloon is to check the time required to use the fuel from one tank. To find out, you can make a flight, running on one tank exclusively, timing how long it takes to exhaust the fuel in that tank. (This should be done only to establish your benchmark time. In practice, a tank should never be emptied; 20 to 30 percent should be saved as a reserve.)

If you have two identical tanks, you will establish how long it takes to use half your fuel. To establish actual time you could fly on a tank, allowing the amount of reserve you prefer, deduct 20 to 30 percent from the time expended to exhaust the tank.

A simple time management plan follows. If you have a two-tank system and like to land with 20 percent reserve, you would inflate the balloon on one tank, fly on that tank until the gauge reads 20 percent, note the time it took to use the first tank, switch to the next tank and be on the ground either when the second tank gauge reads 20 percent or when the allotted time is expended.

Once you have established your benchmark times, you may wish to consider other fuel management plans. Some pilots, with two-burner, two-tank systems, like to switch back and forth between burners, making constant affirmation that both systems are working. You still land at either 20 percent or within your allotted time.

An emergency plan for low fuel with a two-tank system, if a landing site is not found before both tanks are at 20 percent, would be to continue to fly on the last 20 percent of one tank and save the second tank for the actual landing. As the last quarts of propane in a tank are used, the tank pressure decreases. Try to save some normally pressurized fuel for the landing.

Which tank should be saved for the landing? This decision should be made before the flight. Part of your low-fuel plan should take into consideration any differences between tanks. If only one of your tanks supplies fuel to the pilot light and backup system, use that tank last.

The important consideration for pilots to remember is to pay attention, keep records, and always have a plan.

CHAPTER 6

SPECIAL OPERATIONS

This chapter discusses tethering and emergency procedures that are not considered a part of normal flight operations.

TETHERING

Most balloons are designed to be flown free and not tied to the ground. However, in almost every balloonist's life comes an occasion or two when tethering is desired or required. Contrary to the belief of many people, it is much harder to tether a balloon than to fly free.

Considerations

Some important factors to consider before tethering a balloon are the space available, adequate tie-downs, airspace, local ordinances, and crowd control. Also, make sure to check the balloon flight manual for the recommended tethering procedure.

Space Available

The minimum requirement for safely tethering a balloon is a space that contains an area clear of obstacles with a radius twice as wide as the balloon is tall, plus the intended maximum height. For example, if the balloon is 70-feet tall, and you intend to fly 50 feet above the ground, the radius of the area needs to be 190 feet. Then if the balloon was blown down by wind coming from any direction, the balloon would not hit an obstacle.

Tie-Downs

Tie the balloon from the top of the envelope, or use a manufacturer specified tethering harness. To provide stability, the recommended number of lines, from the crown (or harness) and from near the burner frame or basket/envelope interface, should be tied to points on the ground. Some possible tie-downs are heavy vehicles (full-size pickups, vans, or utility vehicles).

The best tie-down material is nylon rope; nylon stretches and is strong. Use a minimum 5/8-inch nylon three-ply twist. Do not use polyester, braided rope or webbing because they do not stretch as much and are not as strong. [Figure 6-1]

Airspace

If you are tethering within Class B, C, or D Airspace, coordinate operations with ATC. Usually a phone call will suffice. ATC may ask you to carry a VHF radio tuned to the tower. Most often a phone call to the controlling agency, and explaining the nature of your operation will be sufficient.

Local Ordinances

Sometimes, due to previous operations by inconsiderate pilots, there may be specific local laws governing balloon operations in a city or county. Make sure you are aware of and comply with such ordinances, or receive a waiver or permission to operate. Perform your legwork, do your homework, and do not be surprised by, or surprise, any authority.

Crowd Control

It is necessary to keep people away from the tether lines and from beneath the basket. It is preferable to keep spectators outside the area formed by the anchor points. Be sure to watch that no one interferes with the anchor points on the ground.

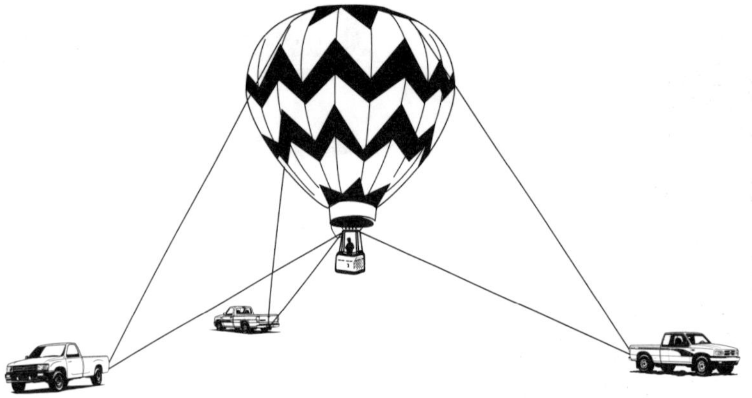

FIGURE 6-1.—Tethering.

Plan ahead in case there is unexpected wind. Tie down correctly to strong anchors, use good ropes, ensure sufficient space, and have adequate crowd control. Tethering a balloon requires experience and should always be done with thought and care.

Tethering vs. Mooring

A tethered balloon is manned and considered an aircraft. Conduct tether operations in accordance with operating, certification, and airworthiness regulations applicable to the aircraft. In order to fly a tethered balloon, you must be an appropriately certificated pilot.

On the other hand, a moored balloon is unmanned and, as such, is not required to be registered or meet any airworthiness standards. Conduct moored balloon operations in accordance with 14 CFR part 101.

EMERGENCY PROCEDURES

Emergency, as defined by a dictionary, is a sudden, unexpected situation or occurrence that requires immediate action. In aviation, an emergency is a critical, possibly life, or property, threatening occurrence that may require outside assistance. To ATC, emergency means that a pilot in command has a problem and must operate the aircraft contrary to ATC instructions. In the case of an emergency, the pilot in command may deviate from a regulation but only to the extent required to meet the emergency. When requested, a written report to the FAA will have to be made, explaining the nature of the deviation.

Emergencies are often not caused by a single problem, but are the result of a series of small events that add up to an emergency. Low fuel is a problem not always recognized as an emergency. Balloon accident reports categorize certain accidents as failure to maintain sufficient altitude, or impact with an obstacle, when the cause of the accident was poor planning on the part of a pilot who made a flight with inadequate fuel.

Planning ahead may help reduce stress when an actual emergency does occur. Every pilot should have a well-planned low-fuel procedure for the occasion when a landing cannot be made at the normal time. Pilots normally land before the fuel gets below 20 percent. You should also have a plan for flying when you cannot find a landing site and your fuel drops below 20 percent. With a multi-tank fuel system, merely deciding in advance which tank will be saved for last could be a stress reliever when the actual low-fuel situation occurs. Most pilots elect to save for last the tank that has (1) the backup system, (2) the most pressure, and (3) the pilot light supply.

Knowing how to operate the balloon heater system without a normal, operating pilot light is a standard emergency operating procedure every pilot should practice. Every pilot should develop the ability to fly without a pilot light (backup, emergency, or other), by igniting the blast flame directly. Experimentation and practice ~~will~~ show that the blast flame should only be ignited when there is a very small flow of propane coming out of the jet. This gives the fuel a chance to mix with air and become flammable. A full-pressure blast of liquid propane will not ignite easily and the cold may extinguish a weak spark. Igniting the blast flame directly is a valuable skill that should be practiced.

Every pilot should know the various ways to operate balloon systems. Even the simplest, single burner system has alternate ways to use the various burners, lines, and tank valves. Know your system. If you are not sure you know your balloon system backwards and forwards, find a good instructor who flies the same make of balloon, and get some instruction on emergency procedures. For your flight reviews, fly with an instructor who knows the make and model of the balloon you fly. If you fly with a different pilot each time, you will get different viewpoints and techniques. If you have an emergency, fly the balloon first and then deal with the problem.

Imagine you are flying along and when you reach up to make a burn, opening of the blast valve makes only a loud hissing sound. Most pilots when asked, "What do you do next?" will answer, "Relight the pilot light." Wrong answer. Since you were trying to make a burn when you discovered the flameout, the first thing is to make a burn. Use a striker, and make the burn. Fly the balloon first, and deal with the problem only if the balloon is under control. The best response to a flameout is (1) make the burn you wanted to make when you discovered the flameout, and (2) check the pilot light valve and tank vapor valve (if fitted) after, or while, making the full-length burn that will keep the balloon flying. The most important thing throughout this process is to fly the balloon.

Pilot light flameout is no longer a frequent problem with modern hot air balloon heater systems, but flameout is an example of a minor problem that can be a major distraction unless the pilot has been trained to fly the balloon.

Another basic rule to remember is that for every propane leak or uncontrolled fire, there is a valve that will turn it off. Some people seem to think a fire extinguisher is the first method of stopping an uncontrolled in-flight fire. The first action to control an in-basket fire is to turn off the valve that controls the burning or leaking fuel. Leaking tanks are so rare as to be almost nonexistent; propane leaks usually come from a loose fitting or an old, cold O-ring. Closing a valve can control both types of leaks.

The most basic emergency equipment is leather gloves and long-sleeved shirts. A few years ago a balloon was totally destroyed, several airplanes damaged, and a field burned, as a result of a small propane vapor leak that started a small fire that could have been extinguished by a pilot wearing gloves. In this case, the pilot, not wearing any protective clothing, jumped out of the basket, during inflation, and ran around looking for a fire extinguisher. Had the pilot been wearing leather gloves, he could have reached into the small flame near the tank vapor valve, turned off the fuel, and prevented the loss of an entire balloon. Always wear gloves.

Another piece of emergency equipment is an ordinary welder's torch igniter, known as a striker. Many modern balloon burners have piezo igniters, but the piezo can be fragile, and usually ignites only the pilot light. If the piezo does not work, or the pilot light system is inoperative, the piezo will be useless. The welder's striker can be used to ignite the main jet flame or the pilot light.

The most common emergency that results in fatalities is balloon contact with powerlines. The most effective defense to avoid powerline contact is altitude. Most powerlines are approximately 30 feet AGL. Powerline towers taller than 120 feet are rare. The most common cause of fatalities during powerline contact is the pilot's attempt to climb over the lines at the last second. The most appropriate action to take, should powerline contact be unavoidable, is deflation. It is far better to make powerline contact with the envelope, than to put the basket, burners, or suspension into the wires. The best advice is see and avoid.

Chapter 7

Regulations and Maintenance

This chapter introduces the balloon pilot to Title 14 of the Code of Federal Regulations (14 CFR) and provides a discussion on required and preventative maintenance.

REGULATIONS

The FAA's mandate from the federal government is to regulate aviation and aeronautics to protect passengers and people on the ground. Title 14 of the Code of Federal Regulations (14 CFR) is designed to promote safety.

Balloon pilots primarily need to be conversant with the following regulations.

- 14 CFR part 1: Definitions and Abbreviations.
- 14 CFR part 31: Airworthiness Standards: Manned Free Balloons.
- 14 CFR part 43: Maintenance, Preventive Maintenance, Rebuilding, and Alteration.
- 14 CFR part 61: Certification: Pilots, Flight Instructors, and Ground Instructors.
- 14 CFR part 91: General Operating and Flight Rules.
- NTSB part 830: Rules Pertaining to the Notification and Reporting of Aircraft Accidents or Incidents and Overdue Aircraft.

Regulations are continually being revised and a good pilot should have some method for keeping up with the latest changes. Some ways to learn regulatory changes are to subscribe to balloon magazines, newsletters, and to attend safety seminars regularly.

Some state and local governments have created laws governing balloon flight and some of these local laws conflict with FAA regulations. It is the responsibility of the pilot to know under what regulations they are operating the balloon. On the ground, the pilot, chase crew, and chase vehicle are subject to local laws. Balloonists should be knowledgeable of local trespass laws, which can vary from area to area.

MAINTENANCE

There are two kinds of maintenance, (1) preventive maintenance, which consists of a specific list of work that may be performed by the owner/operator of an aircraft; and (2) all other maintenance, which must be performed by an authorized repairman at a certificated repair station, a certificated mechanic, or the manufacturer. A well-maintained balloon is safer and easier to fly than a poorly-maintained balloon.

Required Maintenance

Every balloon must have an annual inspection and, if used for commercial purposes, 100-hour inspections. An annual inspection may be performed by a certificated repair station or by a certificated mechanic (A&P) with inspection authorization (IA) who is familiar with the balloon, has the manufacturer's instructions for continued airworthiness, pertinent Airworthiness Directives (ADs), and all required documentation, tools, and equipment.

All manufacturers specify maximum allowable damage in their instructions for continued airworthiness. If the maximum damage is exceeded, the balloon must be repaired before the next flight. Some damage may be repaired by the owner/operator, but most requires repair by certificated personnel.

Service letters and service bulletins are not mandatory but compliance is recommended. ADs are mandatory and must be complied with as directed.

Preventive Maintenance

According to 14 CFR part 43, Appendix A, preventive maintenance may be performed by the owner/operator of an aircraft who holds at least an FAA Private Pilot Certificate with a balloon rating. You may only work on a balloon you own or fly.

The following is a list of preventive maintenance that may be performed by the owner/operator of a balloon.

- Replacing defective safety wiring or cotter keys.
- Lubrication not requiring disassembly.
- The making of small fabric repairs to envelopes (as defined in, and in accordance with, the balloon manufacturers' instructions) not requiring load tape repair or replacement.
- Refinishing decorative coating of the basket when removal or disassembly of any primary structure or operating system is not required.
- Applying preservative or protective material to components where no disassembly of any primary structure or operating system is involved and where such coating is not prohibited or is not contrary to good practices.
- Repairing upholstery and decorative furnishings of the balloon basket interior when the repairing does not require disassembly of any primary structure or operating system or interfere with an operating system or affect primary structure of the aircraft.
- Replacing seats or seat parts with replacement parts approved for the aircraft, not involving disassembly of any primary structure or operating system.
- Replacing prefabricated fuel lines.
- Replacing and servicing batteries.
- Cleaning of balloon burner pilots and main nozzles in accordance with balloon manufacturers' instructions.
- Replacement or adjustment of nonstructural standard fasteners incidental to operations.
- The interchange of balloon baskets and burners on envelopes when the basket or burner is designated as interchangeable in the balloon Type Certificate Data Sheet (TCDS), and the baskets and burners are specifically designed for quick removal and installation.

Any maintenance not specifically listed above must be performed by a certificated aircraft mechanic, repairman or certified repair station, or the manufacturer.

Other Considerations

The following are some considerations that are not usually included under maintenance, but which affect the condition of a balloon.

Storage—The worst enemies of balloon fabric and baskets are moisture, heat, and light. Store your balloon covered in a dry, dark cool place, preferably on a pallet so air can circulate around it. If your balloon is stored in a dry climate for a long period of time, place a plastic bucket of water in the basket and enclose the basket with an opaque cover. The water will raise the humidity near the rattan and keep it flexible. In humid areas you should try to keep the balloon dry to avoid mildew. If you store your balloon in a covered trailer, the trailer should be light-colored, parked in the shade, and ventilated. (A closed, dark trailer sitting in the sun will become an oven, and the heat will degrade the envelope and dry out the basket.)

Handling—The way a balloon is handled will affect its life. Simple things like lowering, not dropping, the balloon from its transport vehicle onto the launch site, and carrying, not dragging it across the ground, will prolong the life of the basket and envelope. Avoid walking on the fabric. The inspection can be done from the mouth and top openings or from a side vent, without walking on fabric. Even shoes may damage fabric coatings.

Volunteer crews may sometimes be necessary, and are often overenthusiastic. Explain to them very carefully your procedure for inflating and packing your balloon. Ask them politely not to step on the fabric, suspension cables, or rattan.

Transportation—If you tie your balloon to a vehicle, or trailer, devise a system that does not crush the wickerwork or the basket edge. Cover the basket to protect it from dirt, ultraviolet, and weather.

Launch/Deflation Site—Check for objects at your inflation/deflation site that may damage the fabric. Clear the site of rocks, glass, and sticks.

Inflation Fan—A large, high-powered fan running at high speed will weaken the fabric in the mouth of a balloon over a period of time. Two-stroke fans, or poorly-maintained fans, will blow pollution into the envelope and shorten fabric life. Prior to using the fan, you should check condition of blades, motor mountings, and security of the blade cage or guard.

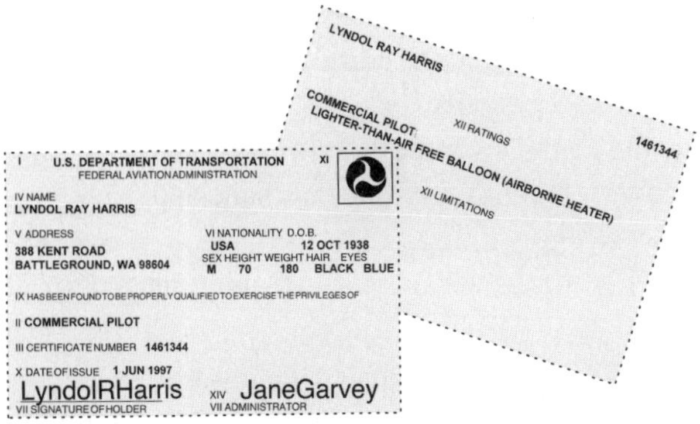

CHAPTER 8

EARNING A PILOT CERTIFICATE

This chapter discusses the requirements for obtaining a pilot certificate, as well as discussing developing pilot skills and the qualities of a good flight instructor.

REQUIREMENTS

Title 14 of the Code of Federal Regulations (14 CFR) part 61 specifies the requirements to earn a pilot certificate.

Eligibility

14 CFR part 61, section 83 establishes the requirements for a student pilot certificate.

To be eligible for a student pilot certificate, an applicant must:

"...(b) Be at least 14 years of age for the operation of a glider or balloon.
(c) Be able to read, speak, write, and understand the English language. If the applicant is unable to meet one of these requirements due to medical reasons, then the Administrator may place such operating limitations on that applicant's pilot certificate as are necessary for the safe operation of the aircraft."

14 CFR part 61, section 61.103, establishes the requirements for a private pilot certificate.

To be eligible for a private pilot certificate, a person must:

"...(b) Be at least 16 years of age for a rating in a glider or balloon.
(c) Be able to read, speak, write, and understand the English language. If the applicant is unable to meet one of these requirements due to medical reasons, then the Administrator may place such operating limitations on that applicant's pilot certificate as are necessary for the safe operation of the aircraft...."
"...(e) Pass the required knowledge test on the aeronautical knowledge areas listed in section 61.105(b) of this part...."
"...(h) Pass a practical test on the areas of operations listed in section 61.107(b) of this part that apply to the aircraft rating sought.
(i) Comply with the appropriate sections of this part that apply to the aircraft category and class rating sought."

14 CFR part 61, section 61.123, establishes the requirements for a commercial pilot certificate.

To be eligible for a commercial pilot certificate, a person must:

"(a) Be at least 18 years of age.
(b) Be able to read, speak, write, and understand the English language. If the applicant is unable to meet one of these requirements due to medical reasons, the Administrator may place such operating limitations on that applicant's pilot certificate as are necessary for the safe operation of the aircraft...."
"...(d) Pass the required knowledge test on the aeronautical knowledge areas listed in section 61.125 of this part;..."

"...(g) Pass the required practical test on the areas of operation listed in section 61.127(b) of this part that apply to the aircraft category and class rating sought;..."
"...(i) Comply with the sections of this part that apply to the aircraft category and class rating sought."

The FAA has specified the aeronautical knowledge and flight proficiency that must be demonstrated to earn a private and commercial certificate as listed below.

Aeronautical Knowledge

Private Pilot

14 CFR part 61, section 61.105.

"(a) *General.* A person who is applying for a private pilot certificate must receive and log ground training from an authorized instructor or complete a home-study course on the aeronautical knowledge areas of paragraph (b) of this section that apply to the aircraft category and class rating sought.
(b) *Aeronautical knowledge areas.*
(1) Applicable Federal Aviation Regulations of this chapter that relate to private pilot privileges, limitations, and flight operations;
(2) Accident reporting requirements of the National Transportation Safety Board;
(3) Use of the applicable portions of the 'Aeronautical Information Manual' and FAA Advisory Circulars;
(4) Use of aeronautical charts for VFR navigation using pilotage, dead reckoning, and navigation systems;
(5) Radio communication procedures;
(6) Recognition of critical weather situations from the ground and in flight, windshear avoidance, and the procurement and use of aeronautical weather reports and forecasts;
(7) Safe and efficient operation of aircraft, including collision avoidance, and recognition and avoidance of wake turbulence;
(8) Effects of density altitude on takeoff and climb performance;
(9) Weight and balance computations;
(10) Principles of aerodynamics, powerplants, and aircraft systems;
(11) Stall awareness, spin entry, spins, and spin recovery techniques for the airplane and glider category ratings;
(12) Aeronautical decision making and judgment; and
(13) Preflight action that includes—
(i) How to obtain information on runway lengths at airports of intended use, data on takeoff and landing distances, weather reports and forecasts, and fuel requirements; and
(ii) How to plan for alternatives if the planned flight cannot be completed or delays are encountered."

Commercial Pilot

14 CFR part 61, section 61.125.

"(a) *General.* A person who applies for a commercial pilot certificate must receive and log ground training from an authorized instructor, or complete a home-study course, on the aeronautical knowledge areas of paragraph (b) of this section that apply to the aircraft category and class rating sought.
(b) Aeronautical knowledge areas.
(1) Applicable Federal Aviation Regulations of this chapter that relate to commercial pilot privileges, limitations, and flight operations;
(2) Accident reporting requirements of the National Transportation Safety Board;
(3) Basic aerodynamics and the principles of flight;
(4) Meteorology to include recognition of critical weather situations, windshear recognition and avoidance, and the use of aeronautical weather reports and forecasts;
(5) Safe and efficient operation of aircraft;
(6) Weight and balance computations;
(7) Use of performance charts;
(8) Significance and effects of exceeding aircraft performance limitations;
(9) Use of aeronautical charts and a magnetic compass for pilotage and dead reckoning;

(10) Use of air navigation facilities;
(11) Aeronautical decision making and judgment;
(12) Principles and functions of aircraft systems;
(13) Maneuvers, procedures, and emergency operations appropriate to the aircraft;
(14) Night and high-altitude operations;
(15) Procedures for operating within the National Airspace System; and
(16) Procedures for flight and ground training for lighter-than-air ratings."

Flight Proficiency

Private Pilot

14 CFR part 61, section 61.107

"(a) *General.* A person who applies for a private pilot certificate must receive and log ground and flight training from an authorized instructor on the areas of operation of this section that apply to the aircraft category and class rating sought.
(b) *Areas of operation.*"
"...(8) For a lighter-than-air category rating with a balloon class rating:
(i) Preflight preparation;
(ii) Preflight procedures;
(iii) Airport operations;
(iv) Launches and landings;
(v) Performance maneuvers;
(vi) Navigation;
(vii) Emergency operations; and
(viii) Postflight procedures."

Commercial Pilot

14 CFR part 61, section 61.127.

"(a) *General.* A person who applies for a commercial pilot certificate must receive and log ground and flight training from an authorized instructor on the areas of operation of this section that apply to the aircraft category and class rating sought.
(b) *Areas of operation.*"
"...(8) For a lighter-than-air category rating with a balloon class rating:
(i) Fundamentals of instructing;
(ii) Technical subjects;
(iii) Preflight preparation;
(iv) Preflight lesson on a maneuver to be performed in flight;
(v) Preflight procedures;
(vi) Airport operations;
(vii) Launches and landings;
(viii) Performance maneuvers;
(ix) Navigation;
(x) Emergency operations; and
(xi) Postflight procedures."

PRACTICAL TEST STANDARDS

Title 14 of the Code of Federal Regulations (14 CFR) part 61 specifies the areas in which knowledge and skill shall be demonstrated by an applicant before issuance of a pilot certificate with the associated category and class ratings. This regulation provides the flexibility that permits the FAA to publish practical test standards containing specific TASKS in which competency shall be demonstrated.

AREAS OF OPERATION are phases of the practical test arranged in a logical sequence. TASKS are knowledge areas, flight procedures, or maneuvers appropriate to an AREA OF OPERATION. However, an examiner may conduct the practical test in any sequence that results in a complete and efficient test.

The tables of contents for the private and commercial balloon practical test standards along with a practical test checklist are presented on the following pages. [Figures 8-1 and 8-2]

CONTENTS

PRIVATE PILOT PRACTICAL TEST STANDARDS FOR LIGHTER-THAN-AIR—BALLOON

1-iii *FAA-S-8081-17*

FIGURE 8-1.—Private Pilot Practical Test Standards (PTS) Excerpt.

V. PERFORMANCE MANEUVERS

VI. NAVIGATION

VII. EMERGENCY OPERATIONS

VIII. POSTFLIGHT PROCEDURES

FAA-S-8081-17 1-iv

FIGURE 8-1.—Private Pilot PTS Excerpt, Continued.

CONTENTS

COMMERCIAL PILOT PRACTICAL TEST STANDARDS FOR LIGHTER-THAN-AIR—BALLOON

FAA-S-8081-18 1-i

FIGURE 8-2.—Commercial Pilot PTS Excerpt.

FIGURE 8-2.—Commercial Pilot PTS Excerpt, Continued.

X. EMERGENCY OPERATIONS

XI. POSTFLIGHT PROCEDURES

NOTE:

LBH—Hot Air Balloon
LBG—Gas Balloon

FIGURE 8-2.—Commercial Pilot PTS Excerpt, Continued.

SKILL DEVELOPMENT

To become a better balloon pilot takes practice, but what should you practice? It is difficult to know because every balloon flight is different. You can improve physical skills by repetitious practice. Do the same thing over and over and you can only get better.

How do you practice when you do not know what direction you will go? How do you practice when you do not know when, where, or how you will land? The fact that there are so many variables in the art of ballooning means you must invent your practice as you go along.

Learning to fly a balloon is similar to learning to drive a car. The beginning driver grips the steering wheel tightly, stares down the road, and works very hard to keep the car between the lines. As the driver becomes more adept, he or she can steer with one hand, carry on a conversation with a passenger, enjoy the scenery, and be much more relaxed while still controlling the car and being a good motorist. Flying a balloon is similar. The better you do it, the more you can enjoy it.

Making tasks for yourself is a way to practice, become a better pilot, and to have fun. For instance, on one flight maybe you will decide to play follow the leader or hare and hound with a friend in another balloon. The other pilot does not even need to know you are trying to follow.

If winds are quite variable, maybe you can make a return flight. You do not necessarily need a box wind to land back at the launch site. Maybe you can contour fly in a direction opposite to the normal prevailing direction, and then when the regular wind starts to come up, fly back to the starting place. It happens.

Even when it is too early to land, you can practice making approaches to landing, "Can I hit that road? Could I land next to that other balloon? Can I fly in the opposite direction of the other balloons? Can I fly 1 foot above the lake without hitting the water?" These are all targets of opportunity—tasks we can use to hone our skills.

Some other tasks to practice are making a rapid descent to a small field for a soft landing, simulating a high-wind landing, climbing or descending at a given rate to a specific altitude, and making a constant-rate descent to a landing.

Flying to a landing site selected before launch, or making a long-distance flight are more ambitious tasks.

Do not give up too soon once you have set a task. If your selected task does not seem possible, stick to it long enough to be sure it was impossible.

Entering and flying in balloon competitions can improve skills. However, dropping a marker on a target is nowhere near as satisfying as being able to land where you choose. Landing a balloon in a safe, legal, appropriate place; however, seems to be a task observed only in a negative way. Many competitions only tell you where not to land. There are some tasks that will help you improve your basic skills, and you always have the right to ignore those that do not.

Your goal is to develop skills that allow you to provide a safe and enjoyable experience for yourself and your passengers.

WHAT IS A GOOD INSTRUCTOR

A good aviation instructor must master many skills and fields of knowledge. What is taught demands technical competence and how the teaching is accomplished depends upon the instructor's understanding of how people learn and the ability to apply that understanding.

The FAA believes that knowledge and understanding, as well as skill, are essential to safety in flight.

Proficient instructors are necessary for the proper development of balloon pilots. Finding the best instructor is a worthwhile goal.

In addition to demonstrating skill in flying a balloon, a good flight instructor must know and practice the principles of safe ballooning, and be able to communicate knowledge and understanding to students.

A training program is dependent upon the quality of the ground and flight instruction the student pilot receives. An instructor should have a thorough understanding of the learning process, knowledge of the fundamentals of teaching, and the ability to communicate effectively with the student pilot.

A good instructor will use a syllabus and insist on correct techniques and procedures from the beginning of training so the student will develop proper habit patterns.

The FAA has several books relative to flight training. However, a good flight instructor should study and be familiar with FAA-H-8083-9, Aviation Instructor's Handbook, which contains information about the psychology of learning and suggested teaching procedures. Balloon Publishing Company's, Balloon Instructor Manual and Balloon Federation of America's, Flight Instructor Manual are also useful tools for the instructor. They contain suggested curriculums and lesson plans, in addition to information on duties and responsibilities and instructions for required endorsements and forms.

Good instructors are active pilots who exercise their skills regularly and continue to learn. A commercial pilot who flies very little each year must spend too much time remembering his or her own skills and procedures to be able to instruct well.

A good instructor keeps current and accurate records for each student. This is required by 14 CFR part 61, and ensures that nothing is omitted from the course of training.

Your instructor should be available to complete your course of training within a reasonable period of time. Training stretched out over many months is far less effective than training completed within a managed period of time. The student often forgets what has been learned and the instructor forgets what has been taught.

One of the most important skills an instructor should possess is the ability to communicate. Use of appropriate language and the selection of terminology help considerably in the transfer of information.

Look for an instructor who has a wide range of knowledge on ballooning. Knowing what reference material is available and where to find it is also important.

Remember that learning is an individual process. An instructor cannot do it for you by pouring knowledge into your head. You can only learn from individual experiences. A good instructor should allow the student to experience the controls at an early stage of flight training. This will give the student a better understanding of what is expected. Too many instructors teach on the principle of "watch me…" A student learning from a hands-on approach will receive better training. As instructors gain confidence and experience, they will improve their ability to transfer their knowledge and skill to students.

CHAPTER 9

AERONAUTICAL DECISION MAKING

INTRODUCTION

Throughout pilot training, safety and good Aeronautical Decision Making (ADM) should be emphasized. This chapter presents some of the basic concepts of ADM to provide an understanding of the process.

GENERAL

Many aeronautical decisions are made easily—like flying on a beautiful day when the weather is perfect. However, some decisions can be more difficult—like whether to terminate the flight when the visibility drops or the wind starts to increase. When this happens, the decision made on whether to continue the flight or land becomes critical to ensuring that the flight is completed safely. All too often many flights end in tragedy because of a bad decision that placed the aircraft in a situation that exceeded the capabilities of the pilot, aircraft, or both. This does not have to happen if a pilot recognizes the importance of timely decision making and takes some of the steps outlined below to ensure that he or she makes the best decisions possible under the circumstances.

Most pilots usually think good judgment is only acquired through years of experience. The average pilot, who flies for pleasure, probably flies a small percentage of the hours that a professional pilot flies over the course of a flying career. A pilot cannot rely simply upon experience as a teacher of good judgment. It is important to learn how to deal with decision making in general and to learn strategies that will lead to effective judgment in a wide variety of situations.

TYPES OF DECISIONS

It is important to recognize that there are two general types of decisions. Decisions that are tied to time constraints and those that are not. In a time constraint decision, a solution is required almost immediately. An example might be if the pilot light went out near the ground. For the most part, a pilot is trained to recognize events like this that require immediate action.

Usually, when time is not a constraint, time is available to gather information and consider alternative courses of action. For example, when planning a flight, a pilot has access to an extensive array of information, such as weather and knowledge of the terrain. A pilot should examine the sources until he or she is confident that all the information needed to make the flight has been examined.

A study conducted by NASA revealed that 80 percent of the errors that led to an incident occurred during the preflight phase, while the actual incidents occurred later during the flight.

It seems obvious that a large number of accidents and incidents could be avoided, if a pilot were to perform better preflight planning. Flight planning is similar to an open-book test in school—all the information needed is available, if a pilot knows where to look. Decision aids are tools that can be used to ensure all relevant information is considered. The appropriate flight planning, followed by the operation of the aircraft within a pilot's capabilities, ensures a safe flight. Good examples of decision making tools are the various checklists that are provided by the manufacturers of aircraft. They are inexpensive, effective, and enhance safety. Checklists provide an effective means of solving the most human of frailties—forgetting. If a pilot follows a checklist, those temporary memory lapses need not have an impact on the flight. The sequence of operations and the critical information required is all recorded for a pilot to use.

EFFECTIVENESS OF ADM

The effectiveness of ADM and the safety of general aviation depend on several factors:

- The knowledge required to understand the situation, the information available, and the possible options.
- The skills required to execute a decision.
- Understanding how to make decisions effectively, including how to search for information and when to stop searching and choose a course of action.
- The self-awareness to recognize when hazardous attitudes are influencing decisions and possessing the self-discipline to overcome those attitudes.

The first two factors, knowledge and skills, will be addressed during ground and flight training. The knowledge required to understand weather conditions, use of checklists, and other items required for flight planning will be explained. An authorized instructor also teaches how to put preflight planning into action. This starts a pilot on a path toward making good aeronautical decisions based on the limitations of the aircraft, weather conditions, and the pilot's experience level. This also helps a pilot develop a positive attitude toward safety and risk management. Having a positive attitude means always considering the potential safety implications of decisions.

Progressive decision making recognizes that changes are constantly taking place, and that a pilot should be continually assessing the outcome. For example, more weather information allows the pilot to judge the quality of the decision and to recognize when it is time to modify that outcome in the face of new information. A pilot with this progressive decision making strategy may make changes rapidly based on the information at hand. The pilot should continue to seek more information about the situation so the plan may be refined and modified if necessary.

Flexibility and the capability to modify actions as new information is obtained are very desirable features of decision making. What this means, in simplest terms, is always having a way out.

The other factor that was mentioned earlier that would affect the quality and safety of a pilot's decisions is attitude. Attitude is one of those aspects of human nature that is hard to define precisely, but we know it when we see it. It is an overall approach to life. It is something in the way people talk and act that makes us think that they are reckless, safe, liberal, conservative, serious, happy-go-lucky, or any one of a number of other adjectives. They have a certain style of responding to life's events that is relatively consistent and which they tend to apply in many situations.

Think for a moment about the stereotypical image of pilots portrayed in popular films—particularly those from several years ago. Films deal in images and an image like that is much easier to portray than the reality. There is a lot of truth to the old adage, "There are old pilots and there are bold pilots, but there are no old, bold pilots." Flying is a wondrous adventure, but it is not the place for boldness, thrill seeking, complacence, or lack of dedication to doing the best one can.

A series of studies conducted a few years ago identified five attitudes among pilots that were particularly hazardous. These attitudes are:

- **Antiauthority—**This attitude is found in people who do not like anyone telling them what to do. Flying is governed by many regulations established for the safety of all, so pilots with this hazardous attitude may rebel against authority by deliberately breaking rules intended for safety.
- **Impulsivity—**This is the attitude of people who frequently feel the need to do something—anything—immediately. They do the first thing that comes to mind, without thinking about what the best alternative might be.
- **Invulnerability**—Many people feel that accidents happen to others, but never to them. They know accidents can happen, and they know that anyone can be affected, but they never really feel or believe they will be personally involved. A pilot with this attitude is more likely to take chances and increase risk.

- **Macho**—A pilot who is always trying to prove that he or she is better than anyone else is thinking, "I can do it—I'll show them." All pilots are equally susceptible to this hazardous attitude which can lead to taking risks to impress others.
- **Resignation—**Pilots who think, "What's the use?" do not see themselves as being able to make a great deal of difference in what happens. They blame whatever happens on luck. Instead of seeking out information and making positive decisions, they just drift along making no changes and hoping for the best.

Having these attitudes can contribute to poor pilot judgment, since they tend to push the pilot toward making decisions that involve more risk. Recognizing that these hazardous attitudes exist is the first step in neutralizing them in the decision making process. Before dismissing these attitudes as belonging to someone else, realize that everyone has these attitudes to some degree. At one time or another all pilots have acted impulsively or in a macho fashion to demonstrate their aviation skills to others.

Pilots should be aware of these attitudes and constantly examine their actions to see if they are falling prey to their influences. This helps a pilot improve the quality of his or her actions.

Developing good decision making skills allows pilots to fly securely in the knowledge that they are controlling risk and ensuring safety. Figure 9-1 provides some useful antidotes for hazardous attitudes.

Minimum Personal Checklist

Proper planning allows a pilot to make better decisions and to have a safer flight. The pilot should not only think in terms of the aircraft, but should consider recency of experience, physical condition, the environment, and external pressures when developing the minimum personal checklist.

HAZARDOUS ATTITUDES	ANTIDOTES
Anti-Authority	Follow the rules. They are usually right.
Impulsivity	Not so fast. Think first.
Invulnerability	It could happen to me.
Macho	Taking chances is foolish.
Resignation	I'm not helpless. I can make a difference.

FIGURE 9-1.—Antidotes for Hazardous Attitudes.

APPENDIX A

SAMPLE WEATHER BRIEFING CHECKLISTS

WEATHER BRIEFING

DATE:______________________ TIME:______________AM/PM

AIRCRAFT NUMBER: N-______________

"AUTOMATED WEATHER"	Wiley Post 495-7192	Will Rogers 682-4871	Westheimer 325-7302
Ceiling	ft.	ft.	ft.
Vis.	miles	miles	miles
Temp.	°C	°C	°C
Dew Point	°C	°C	°C
Wind Dir.	°	°	°
Wind Speed	kts	kts	kts
Baro. Pres.			
Dens. Alt.			

****

"FLIGHT SERVICE" (1-800) WX-BRIEF

Current conditions in flight area: ______________________________

____

____

Surrounding areas: ______________________________

____

____

"WINDS ALOFT FORECAST"

	DIR	SPEED	TEMP
3000 ft.			
6000 ft.			
9000 ft.			

Sunrise: ____________ AM

Sunset: ____________ PM

****

To Talk To A Real Person:

Wiley Post - 798-2040
Will Rogers - 685-0748
Westheimer - 360-9318

NOTES: ______________________________

____

____

____

OAKLAND FSS: 1 800 992 7433 Oakland Direct 510 430 0256

Bay Tape, ext 306; East Tape 303; North Tape 302; Advisories 309; Briefer *99

Time _____:_____ Lcl ___________Z N ____________

"Abbreviated VFR briefing only / Balloon (N#) / local out of Tracy / Dawn / I have Tracy AWOS, Mt. Diablo and Tracy robots / Need the last complete METAR for..."

	Wind	Visblty	Sig WX	Clouds	Temps	Pressure
Oakland OAK	___/___	____	_______	______	___/___	___/___
Travis SUU	___/___	____	_______	______	___/___	___/___
Tracy TCY	___/___	____	_______	______	___/___	___/___
Sacto SMF	___/___	____	_______	______	___/___	___/___
Stockton SCK	___/___	____	_______	______	___/___	___/___
SCK forecast	___/___	______________________				

Winds Aloft	3,000'		6,000'		9,000'	
Bay	______	____	______	____	______	____
Sacramento	______	____	______	____	______	____
Fresno	______	____	______	____	______	____

NOTAMS? PIREPS?

ATIS/AWOS		
Tracy	209 831 4335	119.425
Livermore	510 447 9516	119.65
Modesto	209 526 4555	127.7
Oakland	510 635 5850	128.5
Napa	707 255 2847	124.05
Reid-Hill	408 923 7100	125.2
Sacrmnto	916 648 0679	125.5
Snta Rosa	707 545 2967	135.05
Stockton	209 982 4667	118.25

EMERGENCY 911

P.G.&E. 800 743 5000
800 585 5598

FSS		
Oakland	510 430 0256	122.5
Rcho Mrta	916 354 1561	122.3

ROBOT

Morgan Hill 408 779 6666

Day ________________________________ Date ____________________

MT. DIABLO ROBOT: 510 838 9225 Time: ___:___

The temperature is _____ °C.

Over the past 20 minutes, wind was from	_______	to	_____	Knots
and the average wind is	_______	at	_____	Knots
20 minutes ago, the average wind was	_______	at	_____	Knots
40 minutes ago, the average wind was	_______	at	_____	Knots
60 minutes ago, the average wind was	_______	at	_____	Knots

TRACY AIRPORT AWOS: 209 831 4335 _______ Z Time: ___:___

Sky condition ____________________ Ceiling _______________(Ft. AGL)

Visibility ______________(miles); Temp ________°C; Dew Point ______°C

Wind __________°magnetic at __________knots Peak gusts _____________

Precip. __________ Altimeter _____-_____in. Density Altitude _________

TRACY WIND ROBOT: 209 835 6098

Time	Direction	Knots	Gusts
_______	_______	_______	_______
_______	_______	_______	_______
_______	_______	_______	_______
_______	_______	_______	_______
_______	_______	_______	_______
_______	_______	_______	_______

Confirmation Code _______

Tracy Gate: #4246 UNICOM: 122.8
Tracy Phone Booth 209 835 9938
Tracy Control Tower: 121.2

LVK Phone Booth 510 449 9862
TCY Flight Center 209 835 4266

APPENDIX B

CHECKLISTS

Documentation:	Complete.
Fuel system:	Fuel tank security, clear fuel lines, fuel quantity, leaks, fuel pressure check.
Heater:	Pilot blast valve operating, two igniters.
Deflation port and cooling vent:	Closed.
Deflation and vent lines:	Secure, free.
Suspension lines:	Straight and correct.
Fabric:	No holes exceeding limitations.
Basket:	Loose items secured, drop line attached, tie off and helmets, (if applicable).
Instruments:	Altimeter: set to field elevation or pressure altitude. Pyrometer: within limits. Variometer: at 0.
Crew and passenger briefing:	Complete.

PREFLIGHT CHECKLIST

Inflator fan:	Position fan and begin cold inflation.
Deflation panel:	Check and secure.
Envelope:	Check for damage.
Deflation/vent line:	Check position and security.
Pyrometer probe:	Installed and checked.
Valve line:	Clear of burner flame and secure.
Heater:	Check all clear, light burner, begin heating air.
Envelope mouth:	Ensure fabric and suspension lines are clear of flame during heating.
Crown line:	Secure.
Valve line:	Check for security.
Damage check:	Check envelope, skirt, valve, and suspension lines for damage during inflation.

INFLATION CHECKLIST

Envelope:	Heat to or near equilibrium.
Temperature:	Check envelope temperature reading.
Fuel system:	Check each tank for static and flow pressure.
Instruments:	Check and set.
Passengers:	On board and briefed.
Weather:	Check winds.
Obstacles:	Check around and overhead, ensure adequate clearance for lift-off.

PRE-LAUNCH CHECKLIST

Landing site:	Check wind direction, obstacles, surface condition.
Passengers:	Briefed on facing direction of travel, knees slightly bent, hold on tight, stay in basket.
Equipment:	Secure all loose items, drop line ready, vent/deflation lines clear.
Powerlines:	Observe powerlines in landing area.
Fuel system:	Check best tank, unnecessary valves closed, blast valve off at touchdown.
Landing:	All valves closed, pilot light out, fuel lines empty.

APPROACH/LANDING CHECKLIST

1. Check fuel off, flame out, lines empty.
2. After deflation, monitor envelope until all air out.
3. Disconnect and stow pyrometer wire.
4. Carefully secure deflation line at mouth and pull deflation line to top of envelope, making sure it is not snagged in fabric.
5. Reset velcro or pull parachute to top of envelope.
6. Pack envelope in bag.
7. Disconnect envelope suspension lines, pack on top of skirt.
8. Remove heater.
9. Remove rigid uprights from basket, if applicable.
10. Place envelope, basket, rigid uprights, and heater in chase vehicle.
11. Check field for jackets, gloves, litter.
12. Leave field and gates as found.
13. Thank landowner, if appropriate and available.

RECOVERY/PACK-UP CHECKLIST

1. Gloves on, no nylon clothing.
2. Check that igniters are disabled or removed.
3. Install adapter.
4. Connect adapter to supply hose.
5. Check for leaks by opening tank liquid valve first.
6. Open supply hose valve.
7. Open liquid level indicator valves ¼-turn.
8. Monitor fueling and area.
9. At 90 percent or first "spit," turn off supply valve and then turn off tank valves.
10. Carefully drain supply line.
11. Remove adapter and re-install liquid lines.
12. Check for leaks.

FUELING CHECKLIST

1. Fly with other burner or backup system.
2. Shut off main valve to extinguish fire.
3. Drain fuel line.
4. Use metering valve or tank valve for altitude control.
5. Shut-down burner becomes backup system.
6. Land as soon as practical.

EMERGENCY CHECKLIST—BURNER FIRE

1. Use other burner.
2. Use metering valve as backup pilot light; open ¼-turn or less.
3. Land as soon as practicable.

EMERGENCY CHECKLIST—PILOT LIGHT FAILURE

1. Fly with other burner or backup system.
2. Wiggle handle to dislodge foreign matter or extinguish flame.
3. Shut off appropriate tank valve.
4. Drain fuel line.
5. Use metering valve or tank valve for altitude control.
6. Land as soon as practical.

EMERGENCY CHECKLIST—BLAST VALVE LEAK

1. Confirm all tanks down to 20 percent.
2. Run one tank only while flying to appropriate landing site.
3. Use the fullest tank for final approach and landing.

EMERGENCY CHECKLIST—LOW FUEL

APPENDIX C

PART 31, AIRWORTHINESS STANDARDS: MANNED FREE BALLOONS

Subpart A—General

§31.1 Applicability.

(a) This part prescribes airworthiness standards for the issue of type certificates and changes to those certificates, for manned free balloons.

(b) Each person who applies under Part 21 for such a certificate or change must show compliance with the applicable requirements of this part.

(c) For purposes of this part—

(1) A captive gas balloon is a balloon that derives its lift from a captive lighter-than-air gas;

(2) A hot air balloon is a balloon that derives its lift from heated air;

(3) The envelope is the enclosure in which the lifting means is contained;

(4) The basket is the container, suspended beneath the envelope, for the balloon occupants;

(5) The trapeze is a harness or is a seat consisting of a horizontal bar or platform suspended beneath the envelope for the balloon occupants; and

(6) The design maximum weight is the maximum total weight of the balloon, less the lifting gas or air.

Subpart B—Flight Requirements

§31.12 Proof of compliance.

(a) Each requirement of this subpart must be met at each weight within the range of loading conditions for which certification is requested. This must be shown by—

(1) Tests upon a balloon of the type for which certification is requested or by calculations based on, and equal in accuracy to, the results of testing; and

(2) Systematic investigation of each weight if compliance cannot be reasonably inferred from the weights investigated.

(b) Except as provided in §31.17(b), allowable weight tolerances during flight testing are +5 percent and -10 percent.

§31.14 Weight limits.

(a) The range of weights over which the balloon may be safely operated must be established.

(b) *Maximum weight.* The maximum weight is the highest weight at which compliance with each applicable requirement of this part is shown. The maximum weight must be established so that it is not more than—

(1) The highest weight selected by the applicant;

(2) The design maximum weight which is the highest weight at which compliance with each applicable structural loading condition of this part is shown; or

(3) The highest weight at which compliance with each applicable flight requirement of this part is shown.

(c) The information established under paragraphs (a) and (b) of this section must be made available to the pilot in accordance with §31.81.

§31.16 Empty weight.

The empty weight must be determined by weighing the balloon with installed equipment but without lifting gas or heater fuel.

§31.17 Performance: Climb.

(a) Each balloon must be capable of climbing at least 300 feet in the first minute after takeoff with a steady rate of climb. Compliance with the requirements of this section must be shown at each altitude and ambient temperature for which approval is sought.

(b) Compliance with the requirements of paragraph (a) of this section must be shown at the maximum weight with a weight tolerance of +5 percent.

§31.19 Performance: Uncontrolled descent.

(a) The following must be determined for the most critical uncontrolled descent that can result from any single failure of the heater assembly, fuel cell system, gas value system, or maneuvering vent system, or from any single tear in the balloon envelope between tear stoppers:

(1) The maximum vertical velocity attained.

(2) The altitude loss from the point of failure to the point at which maximum vertical velocity is attained.

(3) The altitude required to achieve level flight after corrective action is initiated, with the balloon descending at the maximum vertical velocity determined in paragraph (a)(1) of this section.

(b) Procedures must be established for landing at the maximum vertical velocity determined in paragraph (a)(1) of this section and for arresting that descent rate in accordance with paragraph (a)(3) of this section.

§31.20 Controllability.

The applicant must show that the balloon is safely controllable and maneuverable during takeoff, ascent, descent, and landing without requiring exceptional piloting skill.

Subpart C—Strength Requirements

§31.21 Loads.

Strength requirements are specified in terms of limit loads, that are the maximum load to be expected in service, and ultimate loads, that are limit loads multiplied by prescribed factors of safety. Unless otherwise specified, all prescribed loads are limit loads.

§31.23 Flight load factor.

In determining limit load, the limit flight load factor must be at least 1.4.

§31.25 Factor of safety.

(a) Except as specified in paragraphs (b) and (c) of this section, the factor of safety is 1.5.

(b) A factor of safety of at least five must be used in envelope design. A reduced factor of safety of at least two may be used if it is shown that the selected factor will preclude failure due to creep or instantaneous rupture from lack of rip stoppers. The selected factor must be applied to the more critical of the maximum operating pressure or envelope stress.

(c) A factor of safety of at least five must be used in the design of all fibrous or non-metallic parts of the rigging and related attachments of the envelope to basket, trapeze, or other means provided for carrying occupants. The primary attachments of the envelope to the basket, trapeze, or other means provided for carrying occupants must be designed so that failure is extremely remote or so that any single failure will not jeopardize safety of flight.

(d) In applying factors of safety, the effect of temperature, and other operating characteristics, or both, that may affect strength of the balloon must be accounted for.

(e) For design purposes, an occupant weight of at least 170 pounds must be assumed.

§31.27 Strength.

(a) The structure must be able to support limit loads without detrimental effect.

(b) The structure must be substantiated by test to be able to withstand the ultimate loads for at least three seconds without failure. For the envelope, a test of a representative part is acceptable, if the part tested is large enough to include critical seams, joints, and load attachment points and members.

(c) An ultimate free-fall drop test must be made of the basket, trapeze, or other place provided for occupants. The test must be made at design maximum weight on a horizontal surface, with the basket, trapeze, or other means provided for carrying occupants, striking the surface at angles of 0, 15, and 30 degrees. The weight may be distributed to simulate actual conditions. There must be no distortion or failure that is likely to cause serious injury to the occupants. A drop test height of 36 inches, or a drop test height that produces, upon impact, a velocity equal to the maximum vertical velocity determined in accordance with §31.19, whichever is higher, must be used.

Subpart D—Design Construction

§31.31 General.

The suitability of each design detail or part that bears on safety must be established by tests or analysis.

§31.33 Materials.

(a) The suitability and durability of all materials must be established on the basis of experience or tests. Materials must conform to approved specifications that will ensure that they have the strength and other properties assumed in the design data.

(b) Material strength properties must be based on enough tests of material conforming to specifications so as to establish design values on a statistical basis.

§31.35 Fabrication methods.

The methods of fabrication used must produce a consistently sound structure. If a fabrication process requires close control to reach this objective, the process must be performed in accordance with an approved process specification.

§31.37 Fastenings.

Only approved bolts, pins, screws, and rivets may be used in the structure. Approved locking devices or methods must be used for all these bolts, pins, and screws, unless the installation is shown to be free from vibration. Self-locking nuts may not be used on bolts that are subject to rotation in service.

§31.39 Protection

Each part of the balloon must be suitably protected against deterioration or loss of strength in service due to weathering, corrosion, or other causes.

§31.41 Inspection provisions.

There must be a means to allow close examination of each part that require repeated inspection and adjustment.

§31.43 Fitting factor.

(a) A fitting factor of at least 1.15 must be used in the analysis of each fitting the strength of which is not proven by limit and ultimate load tests in which the actual stress conditions are simulated in the fitting and surrounding structure. This factor applies to all parts of the fitting, the means of attachment, and the bearing on the members joined.

(b) Each part with an integral fitting must be treated as a fitting up to the point where the section properties become typical of the member.

(c) The fitting factor need not be used if the joint design is made in accordance with approved practices and is based on comprehensive test data.

§31.45 Fuel cells.

If fuel cells are used, the fuel cells, their attachments, and related supporting structure must be shown by tests to be capable of withstanding, without detrimental distortion or failure, any inertia loads to which the installation may be subjected, including the drop tests prescribed in §31.27(c). In the tests, the fuel cells must be loaded to the weight and pressure equivalent to the full fuel quantity condition.

§31.46 Pressurized fuel systems.

For pressurized fuel systems, each element and its connecting fittings and lines must be tested to an ultimate pressure of at least twice the maximum pressure to which the system will be subjected in normal operation. No part of the system may fail or malfunction during the test. The test configuration must be representative of the normal fuel system installation and balloon configuration.

§31.47 Heaters.

(a) If a heater is used to provide the lifting means, the system must be designed and installed so as not to create a fire hazard.

(b) There must be shielding to protect parts adjacent to the burner flame, and the occupants, from heater effects.

(c) There must be controls, instruments, or other equipment essential to the safe control and operation of the heater. They must be shown to be able to perform their intended functions during normal and emergency operation.

(d) The heater system (including the burner unit, controls, fuel lines, fuel cells, regulators, control valves, and other related elements) must be substantiated by an endurance test of at least 50 hours. In making the test, each element of the system must be installed and tested so as to simulate the actual balloon installation. The test program must be conducted so that each 10-hour part of the test includes 7 hours at maximum heat output of the heater and 3 hours divided into a least 10 equal increments between minimum and maximum heat output ranges.

(e) The test must also include at least three flameouts and restarts.

(f) Each element of the system must be serviceable at the end of the test.

§31.49 Control systems.

(a) Each control must operate easily, smoothly, and positively enough to allow proper performance of its functions. Controls must be arranged and identified to provide for convenience of operation and to prevent the possibilities of confusion and subsequent inadvertent operation.

(b) Each control system and operating device must be designed and installed in a manner that will prevent jamming, chafing, or interference from passengers, cargo, or loose objects. Precaution must be taken to prevent foreign objects from jamming the controls. The elements of the control system must have design features or must be distinctly and permanently marked to minimize the possibility of incorrect assembly that could result in malfunctioning of the control system.

(c) Each balloon using a captive gas as the lifting means must have an automatic valve or appendix that is able to release gas automatically at the rate of at least three percent of the total volume per minute when the balloon is at its maximum operating pressure.

(d) Each hot air balloon must have a means to allow the controlled release of hot air during flight.

(e) Each hot air balloon must have a means to indicate the maximum envelope skin temperatures occurring during operation. The indicator must be readily visible to the pilot and marked to indicate the limiting safe temperature of the envelope material. If the markings are on the cover glass of the instrument, there must be provisions to maintain the correct alignment of the glass cover with the face of the dial.

§31.51 Ballast.

Each captive gas balloon must have a means for the safe storage and controlled release of ballast. The ballast must consist of material that, if released during flight, is not hazardous to persons on the ground.

§31.53 Drag rope.

If a drag rope is used, the end that is released overboard must be stiffened to preclude the probability of the rope becoming entangled with trees, wires, or other objects on the ground.

§31.55 Deflation means.

There must be a means to allow emergency deflation of the envelope so as to allow a safe emergency landing. If a system other than a manual system is used, the reliability of the system used must be substantiated.

§31.57 Rip cords.

(a) If a rip cord is used for emergency deflation, it must be designed and installed to preclude entanglement.

(b) The force required to operate the rip cord may not be less than 25, or more than 75, pounds.

(c) The end of the rip cord to be operated by the pilot must be colored red.

(d) The rip cord must be long enough to allow an increase of at least 10 percent in the vertical dimension of the envelope.

§31.59 Trapeze, basket, or other means provided for occupants.

(a) The trapeze, basket, or other means provided for carrying occupants may not rotate independently of the envelope.

(b) Each projecting object on the trapeze, basket, or other means provided for carrying occupants, that could cause injury to the occupants, must be padded.

§31.61 Static discharge.

Unless shown not to be necessary for safety, there must be appropriate bonding means in the design of each balloon using flammable gas as a lifting means to ensure that the effects of static discharges will not create a hazard.

§31.63 Safety belts.

(a) There must be a safety belt, harness, or other restraining means for each occupant, unless the Administrator finds it unnecessary. If installed, the belt, harness, or other restraining means and its supporting structure must meet the strength requirements of Subpart C of this part.

(b) This section does not apply to balloons that incorporate a basket or gondola.

§31.65 Position lights.

(a) If position lights are installed, there must be one steady aviation white position light and one flashing aviation red (or flashing aviation white) position light with an effective flash frequency of at least 40, but not more than 100, cycles per minute.

(b) Each light must provide 360° horizontal coverage at the intensities prescribed in this paragraph. The following light intensities must be determined with the light source operating at a steady state and with all light covers and color filters in place and at the manufacturer's rated minimum voltage. For the flashing aviation red light, the measured values must be adjusted to correspond to a red filter temperature of at least 130:

(1) The intensities in the horizontal plane passing through the light unit must equal or exceed the following values:

Position light	Minimum intensity (candles)
Steady white	20
Flashing red or white	40

(2) The intensities in vertical planes must equal or exceed the following values. An intensity of one unit corresponds to the applicable horizontal plane intensity specified in paragraph (b)(1) of this section.

Angles above and below the horizontal in any vertical plane (degrees)	Minimum intensity (units)
0	1.00
0 to 5	0.90
5 to 10	0.80
10 to 15	0.70
15 to 20	0.50
20 to 30	0.30
30 to 40	0.10
40 to 60	0.05

(c) The steady white light must be located not more than 20 feet below the basket, trapeze, or other means for carrying occupants. The flashing red or white light must be located not less than 7, nor more than 10, feet below the steady white light.

(d) There must be a means to retract and store the lights.

(e) Each position light color must have the applicable International Commission on Illumination chromaticity coordinates as follows:

(1) *Aviation red*—
"y" is not greater than 0.335; and "z" is not greater than 0.002.

(2) *Aviation white*—
"x" is not less than 0.300 and not greater than 0.540;
"y" is not less than "x"-0.040" or "y_0-0.010", whichever is the smaller; and
"y" is not greater than "x+0.020" nor "0.636-0.0400 x";
Where "y_0" is the "y" coordinate of the Planckian radiator for the value of "x" considered.

Subpart E—Equipment

§31.71 Function and installation.

(a) Each item of installed equipment must—

(1) Be of a kind and design appropriate to its intended function;

(2) Be permanently and legibly marked or, if the item is too small to mark, tagged as to its identification, function, or operating limitations, or any applicable combination of those factors;

(3) Be installed according to limitations specified for that equipment; and

(4) Function properly when installed.

(b) No item of installed equipment, when performing its function, may affect the function of any other equipment so as to create an unsafe condition.

(c) The equipment, systems, and installations must be designed to prevent hazards to the balloon in the event of a probable malfunction or failure.

Subpart F—Operating Limitations and Information

§31.81 General.

(a) The following information must be established:

(1) Each operating limitation, including the maximum weight determined under §31.14.

(2) The normal and emergency procedures.

(3) Other information necessary for safe operation, including—

(i) The empty weight determined under §31.16;

(ii) The rate of climb determined under §31.17, and the procedures and conditions used to determine performance;

(iii) The maximum vertical velocity, the altitude drop required to attain that velocity, and altitude drop required to recover from a descent at that velocity, determined under §31.19, and the procedures and conditions used to determine performance; and

(iv) Pertinent information peculiar to the balloon's operating characteristics.

(b) The information established in compliance with paragraph (a) of this section must be furnished by means of—

(1) A Balloon Flight Manual; or

(2) A placard on the balloon that is clearly visible to the pilot.

§31.82 Instructions for Continued Airworthiness.

The applicant must prepare Instructions for Continued Airworthiness in accordance with Appendix A to this part that are acceptable to the Administrator. The instructions may be incomplete at type certification if a program exists to ensure their completion prior to delivery of the first balloon or issuance of a standard certificate of airworthiness, whichever occurs later.

§31.83 Conspicuity.

The exterior surface of the envelope must be of a contrasting color or colors so that it will be conspicuous during operation. However, multicolored banners or streamers are acceptable if it can be shown that they are large enough, and there are enough of them of contrasting color, to make the balloon conspicuous during flight.

§31.85 Required basic equipment.

In addition to any equipment required by this subchapter for a specific kind of operation, the following equipment is required:

(a) For all balloons:

(1) [Reserved]

(2) An altimeter.

(3) A rate of climb indicator.

(b) For hot air balloons:

(1) A fuel quantity gauge. If fuel cells are used, means must be incorporated to indicate to the crew the quantity of fuel in each cell during flight. The means must be calibrated in appropriate units or in percent of fuel cell capacity.

(2) An envelope temperature indicator.

(c) For captive gas balloons, a compass.

APPENDIX A TO PART 31— INSTRUCTIONS FOR CONTINUED AIRWORTHINESS

A31.1 GENERAL

(a) This appendix specifies requirements for the preparation of Instructions for Continued Airworthiness as required by §31.82.

(b) The Instructions for Continued Airworthiness for each balloon must include the Instructions for Continued Airworthiness for all balloon parts required by this chapter and required information relating to the interface of those parts with the balloon. If instructions for Continued Airworthiness are not supplied by the part manufacturer for a balloon part, the Instructions for Continued Airworthiness for the balloon must include the information essential to the continued airworthiness of the balloon.

(c) The applicant must submit to the FAA a program to show how changes to the Instructions for Continued Airworthiness made by the applicant or by the manufacturers of balloon parts will be distributed.

A31.2 FORMAT

(a) The Instructions for Continued Airworthiness must be in the form of a manual or manuals as appropriate for the quantity of data to be provided.

(b) The format of the manual or manuals must provide for a practical arrangement.

A31.3 CONTENT

The contents of the manual or manuals must be prepared in the English language. The Instructions for Continued Airworthiness must contain the following information:

(a) Introduction information that includes an explanation of the balloon's features and data to the extent necessary for maintenance or preventive maintenance.

(b) A description of the balloon and its systems and installations.

(c) Basic control and operation information for the balloon and its components and systems.

(d) Servicing information that covers details regarding servicing of balloon components, including burner nozzles, fuel tanks and valves during operations.

(e) Maintenance information for each part of the balloon and its envelope, controls, rigging, basket structure, fuel systems, instruments, and heater assembly that provides the recommended periods at which they should be cleaned, adjusted, tested, and lubricated, the applicable wear tolerances, and the degree of work recommended at these periods. However, the applicant may refer to an accessory, instrument, or equipment manufacturer as the source of this information if the applicant shows that the item has an exceptionally high degree of complexity requiring specialized maintenance techniques, test equipment, or expertise. The recommended overhaul periods and necessary cross references to the Airworthiness Limitations section of the manual must also be included. In addition, the applicant must include an inspection program that includes the frequency and extent of the inspections necessary to provide for the continued airworthiness of the balloon.

(f) Troubleshooting information describing probable malfunctions, how to recognize those malfunctions, and the remedial action for those malfunctions.

(g) Details of what, and how, to inspect after a hard landing.

(h) Instructions for storage preparation including storage limits.

(i) Instructions for repair on the balloon envelope and its basket or trapeze.

A31.4 AIRWORTHINESS LIMITATIONS SECTION

The Instructions for Continued Airworthiness must contain a section titled Airworthiness Limitations that is segregated and clearly distinguishable from the rest of the document. This section must set forth each mandatory replacement time, structural inspection interval, and related structural inspection procedure, including envelope structural integrity, required for type certification. If the Instructions for Continued Airworthiness consist of multiple documents, the section required by this paragraph must be included in the principal manual. This section must contain a legible statement in a prominent location that reads: "The Airworthiness Limitations section is FAA approved and specifies maintenance required under §§43.16 and 91.403 of the Federal Aviation Regulations."

APPENDIX D

AIRMAN APPLICATION

AIRMAN CERTIFICATE AND/OR RATING APPLICATION
INSTRUCTIONS FOR COMPLETING FAA FORM 8710-1

I. APPLICATION INFORMATION. *Check appropriate blocks(s).*

Block A. Name. Enter legal name. Use no more than one middle name for record purposes. Do not change the name on subsequent applications unless it is done in accordance with 14 CFR Section 61.25. If you do not have a middle name, enter "NMN". If you have a middle initial only, indicate "Initial only." If you are a Jr., or a II, or III, so indicate. If you have an FAA certificate, the name on the application should be the same as the name on the certificate unless you have had it changed in accordance with 14 CFR Section 61.25.

Block B. Social Security Number. Optional: See supplemental Information Privacy Act. Do not leave blank: Use only **US Social Security Number**. Enter either "SSN" or the words "Do not Use" or "None." SSN's are not shown on certificates.

Block C. Date of Birth. Check for accuracy. Enter eight digits; Use numeric characters, i.e., 07-09-1925 instead of July 9, 1925. Check to see that DOB is the same as it is on the medical certificate.

Block D. Place of Birth. If you were born in the USA, enter the city and state where you were born. If the city is unknown, enter the county and state. If you were born outside the USA, enter the name of the city and country where you were born.

Block E. Permanent Mailing Address. Enter residence number and street, P.O. Box or rural route number in the top part of the block above the line. The City, State, and ZIP code go in the bottom part of the block below the line. Check for accuracy. Make sure the numbers are not transposed. FAA policy requires that you use your permanent mailing address. **Justification must be provided on a separate sheet of paper signed and submitted with the application when a PO Box or rural route number is used in place of your permanent physical address. A map or directions must be provided if a physical address is unavailable.**

Block F. Citizenship. Check USA if applicable. If not, enter the country where you are a citizen.

Block G. Do you read, speak, write and understand the English language? Check yes or no.

Block H. Height. Enter your height in inches. Example: 5'8" would be entered as 68 in. No fractions, use whole inches only.

Block I. Weight. Enter your weight in pounds. No fractions, use whole pounds only.

Block J. Hair. Spell out the color of your hair. If bald, enter "Bald." Color should be listed as black, red, brown, blond, or gray. If you wear a wig or toupee, enter the color of your hair under the wig or toupee.

Block K. Eyes. Spell out the color of your eyes. The color should be listed as blue, brown, black, hazel, green, or gray.

Block L. Sex. Check male or female.

Block M. Do You Now Hold or Have You Ever Held An FAA Pilot Certificate? Check yes or no. (NOTE: A student pilot certificate is a "Pilot Certificate.")

Block N. Grade of Pilot Certificate. Enter the grade of pilot certificate (i.e., Student, Recreational, Private, Commercial, or ATP). Do NOT enter flight instructor certificate information.

Block O. Certificate Number. Enter the number as it appears on your pilot certificate.

Block P. Date Issued. Enter the date your pilot certificate was issued.

Block Q. Do You Now Hold A Medical Certificate? Check yes or no. If yes, complete Blocks R, S, and T.

Block R. Class of Certificate. Enter the class as shown on the medical certificate, i.e., 1st, 2nd, or 3rd class.

Block S. Date Issued. Enter the date your medical certificate was issued.

Block T. Name of Examiner. Enter the name as shown on medical certificate.

Block U. Narcotics, Drugs. Check appropriate block. Only check "Yes" if you have actually been convicted. If you have been charged with a violation which has not been adjudicated, check ."No".

Block V. Date of Final Conviction. If block "U" was checked "Yes" give the date of final conviction.

II. CERTIFICATE OR RATING APPLIED FOR ON BASIS OF:

Block A. Completion of Required Test.

1. AIRCRAFT TO BE USED. (If flight test required) – Enter the make and model of each aircraft used. If simulator or FTD, indicate.
2. TOTAL TIME IN THIS AIRCRAFT (Hrs.) – (a) Enter the total Flight Time in each make and model. (b) Pilot-In-Command Flight Time - In each make and model.

Block B. Military Competence Obtained In. Enter your branch of service, date rated as a military pilot, your rank, or grade and service number. In block 4a or 4b, enter the make and model of each military aircraft used to qualify (as appropriate).

Block C. Graduate of Approved Course.

1. NAME AND LOCATION OF TRAINING AGENCY/CENTER. As shown on the graduation certificate. Be sure the location is entered.
2. AGENCY SCHOOL/CENTER CERTIFICATION NUMBER. As shown on the graduation certificate. Indicate if 142 training center.
3. CURRICULUM FROM WHICH GRADUATED. As shown on the graduation certificate.
4. DATE. Date of graduation from indicated course. Approved course graduate must also complete Block "A" COMPLETION OF REQUIRED TEST.

Block D. Holder of Foreign License Issued By.

1. COUNTRY. Country which issued the license.
2. GRADE OF LICENSE. Grade of license issued, i.e., private, commercial, etc.
3. NUMBER. Number which appears on the license.
4. RATINGS. All ratings that appear on the license.

Block E. Completion of Air Carrier's Approved Training Program.

1. Name of Air Carrier.
2. Date program was completed.
3. Identify the Training Curriculum.

III. RECORD OF PILOT TIME.

The minimum pilot experience required by the appropriate regulation must be entered. It is recommended, however, that ALL pilot time be entered. If decimal points are used, be sure they are legible. Night flying must be entered when required. You should fill in the blocks that apply and ignore the blocks that do not. Second In Command "SIC" time used may be entered in the appropriate blocks. Flight Simulator, Flight Training Device and PCATD time may be entered in the boxes provided. Total, Instruction received, and Instrument Time should be entered in the top, middle, or bottom of the boxes provided as appropriate.

IV. HAVE YOU FAILED A TEST FOR THIS CERTIFICATE OR RATING?

Check appropriate block.

V. APPLICANT'S CERTIFICATION.

A. SIGNATURE. The way you normally sign your name.
B. DATE. The date you sign the application.

TYPE OR PRINT ALL ENTRIES IN INK

Form Approved OMB No: 2120-0021

DEPARTMENT OF TRANSPORTATION
FEDERAL AVIATION ADMINISTRATION

Airman Certificate and/or Rating Application

I. Application Information ☐ Student ☐ Recreational ☐ Private ☐ Commercial ☐ Airline Transport ☐ Instrument
☐ Additional Rating ☐ Airplane Single-Engine ☐ Airplane Multiengine ☐ Rotorcraft ☐ Balloon ☐ Airship ☐ Glider ☐ Powered-Lift
☐ Flight Instructor ____ Initial ____ Renewal ____ Reinstatement ☐ Additional Instructor Rating ☐ Ground Instructor
☐ Medical Flight Test ☐ Reexamination ☐ Reissuance of ______________ certificate ☐ Other ______

A. Name (Last, First, Middle)	B. SSN (US Only)	C. Date of Birth Month Day Year	D. Place of Birth
E. Address	F. Citizenship ☐ USA ☐ Other ______ Specify	G. Do you read, speak, write, & understand the English language? ☐ Yes ☐ No	
City, State, Zip Code	H. Height / I. Weight / J. Hair	K. Eyes	L. Sex ☐ Male ☐ Female
M. Do you now hold, or have you ever held an FAA Pilot Certificate? ☐ Yes ☐ No	N. Grade Pilot Certificate	O. Certificate Number	P. Date Issued
Q. Do you hold a Medical Certificate? ☐ Yes ☐ No / R. Class of Certificate	S. Date Issued	T. Name of Examiner	
U. Have you ever been convicted for violation of any Federal or State statutes relating to narcotic drugs, marijuana, or depressant or stimulant drugs or substances? ☐ Yes ☐ No			V. Date of Final Conviction

II. Certificate or Rating Applied For on Basis of:

☐ A. Completion of Required Test	1. Aircraft to be used (if flight test required)	2a. Total time in this aircraft / SIM / FTD hours	2b. Pilot in command hours
☐ B. Military Competence Obtained In	1. Service	2. Date Rated	3. Rank or Grade and Service Number
	4a. Flown 10 hours PIC in last 12 months in the following Military Aircraft.	4b. US Military PIC & Instrument check in last 12 months (List Aircraft)	
☐ C. Graduate of Approved Course	1. Name and Location of Training Agency or Training Center		1a. Certification Number
	2. Curriculum From Which Graduated		3. Date
☐ D. Holder of Foreign License Issued By	1. Country	2. Grade of License	3. Number
	4. Ratings		
☐ E. Completion of Air Carrier's Approved Training Program	1. Name of Air Carrier	2. Date	3. Which Curriculum ☐ Initial ☐ Upgrade ☐ Transition

III RECORD OF PILOT TIME (Do not write in the shaded areas.)

	Total	Instruction Received	Solo	Pilot in Command (PIC)	Cross Country Instruction Received	Cross Country Solo	Cross Country PIC	Instrument	Night Instruction Received	Night Take-off/ Landings	Night PIC	Night Take-Off/ Landing PIC	Number of Flights	Number of Aero-Tows	Number of Ground Launches	Number of Powered Launches
Airplanes				PIC / SIC			PIC / SIC				PIC / SIC	PIC / SIC				
Rotorcraft				PIC / SIC			PIC / SIC				PIC / SIC	PIC / SIC				
Powered Lift				PIC / SIC			PIC / SIC				PIC / SIC	PIC / SIC				
Gliders																
Lighter Than Air																
Simulator																
Training Device																
PCATD																

IV. Have you failed a test for this certificate or rating? ☐ Yes ☐ No

V. Applicants's Certification -- I certify that all statements and answers provided by me on this application form are complete and true to the best of my knowledge and I agree that they are to be considered as part of the basis for issuance of any FAA certificate to me. I have also read and understand the Privacy Act statement that accompanies this form.

Signature of Applicant	Date

FAA Form 8710-1 (4-00) Supersedes Previous Edition

NSN: 0052-00-682-5007

Instructor's Recommendation

I have personally instructed the applicant and consider this person ready to take the test.

Date	Instructor's Signature (Print Name & Sign)	Certificate No:	Certificate Expires

Air Agency's Recommendation

The applicant has successfully completed our ______________________ course, and is recommended for certification or rating without further ______________________ test.

Date	Agency Name and Number	Officials Signature
		Title

Designated Examiner or Airman Certification Representative Report

- ☐ Student Pilot Certificate Issued (Copy attached)
- ☐ I have personally reviewed this applicant's pilot logbook and/or training record, and certify that the individual meets the pertinent requirements of 14 CFR Part 61 for the certificate or rating sought.
- ☐ I have personally reviewed this applicant's graduation certificate, and found it to be appropriate and in order, and have returned the certificate.
- ☐ I have personally tested and/or verified this applicant in accordance with pertinent procedures and standards with the result indicated below.
  - ☐ Approved -- Temporary Certificate Issued (Original Attached)
  - ☐ Disapproved -- Disapproval Notice Issued (Original Attached)

Location of Test (Facility, City, State)	Duration of Test		
	Ground	Simulator/FTD	Flight

Certificate or Rating for Which Tested	Type(s) of Aircraft Used	Registration No.(s)

Date	Examiner's Signature (Print Name & Sign)	Certificate No.	Designation No.	Designation Expires

Evaluator's Record (Use For ATP Certificate and/or Type Ratings)

	Inspector	Examiner	Signature and Certificate Number	Date
Oral	☐	☐	____________	____________
Approved Simulator/Training Device Check	☐	☐	____________	____________
Aircraft Flight Check	☐	☐	____________	____________
Advanced Qualification Program	☐	☐	____________	____________

Aviation Safety Inspector or Technician Report

I have personally tested this applicant in accordance with or have otherwise verified that this applicant complies with pertinent procedures, standards, policies, and or necessary requirements with the result indicated below.

☐ Approved -- Temporary Certificate Issued (Original Attached) ☐ Disapproved -- Disapproval Notice Issued (Original Attached)

Location of Test (Facility, City, State)	Duration of Test		
	Ground	Simulator/FTD	Flight

Certificate or Rating for Which Tested	Type(s) of Aircraft Used	Registration No.(s)

- ☐ Student Pilot Certificate Issued
- ☐ Examiner's Recommendation
  - ☐ Accepted ☐ Rejected
- ☐ Reissue or Exchange of Pilot Certificate
- ☐ Special Medical test conducted -- report forwarded to Aeromedical Certification Branch, AAM-330

- ☐ Certificate or Rating Based on
  - ☐ Military Competence
  - ☐ Foreign License
  - ☐ Approved Course Graduate
  - ☐ Other Approved FAA Qualification Criteria

- ☐ Flight Instructor ☐ Ground Instructor
  - ☐ Renewal
  - ☐ Reinstatement
- Instructor Renewal Based on
  - ☐ Activity ☐ Training Course
  - ☐ Test ☐ Duties and Responsibilities

Training Course (FIRC) Name	Graduation Certificate No.	Date

Date	Inspector's Signature (Print Name & Sign)	Certificate No.	FAA District Office

Attachments:

- ☐ Student Pilot Certificate (Copy)
- ☐ Knowledge Test Report
- ☐ Temporary Airman Certificate
- ☐ Notice of Disapproval
- ☐ Superseded Airman Certificate

☐ Airman's Identification (ID)

____
Form of ID

____
Number

____
Expiration Date

____
Telephone Number

ID:
Name: ______________________

Date of Birth: ______________________

Certificate Number: ______________________

E-Mail Address ______________________

FAA Form 8710-1 (4-00) Supersedes Previous Edition

NSN: 0052-00-682-5007

GLOSSARY

GLOSSARY

Abeam—A relative location approximately at right angles to the logitudinal axis of an aircraft.

Abort—To terminate an operation prematurely when it is seen that the desired result will not occur.

Absolute Altitude—The actual distance between an aircraft and the terrain over which it is flying.

AC (Advisory Circular)—An FAA publication that informs the aviation public, in a systematic way, of nonregulatory material.

AC 43.13-1A—An advisory circular in book form issued by the FAA, giving examples of acceptable methods, techniques, and practices for aircraft inspection and repair.

Accident—An occurrence associated with the operation of an aircraft which takes place between the time any person boards the aircraft with the intention of flight and all such persons have disembarked, and in which any person suffers death or serious injury, or in which the aircraft receives substantial damage. (NTSB 830.2)

AD (Airworthiness Directive)—A regulatory notice sent out by the FAA to the registered owner of an aircraft informing him or her of a condition that prevents the aircraft from meeting its conditions for airworthiness. Compliance requirements will be stated in the AD.

Administrator—The FAA Administrator or any person to whom he or she has delegated authority in the matter concerned.

Aeronaut—A person who operates or travels in a balloon or airship.

Aeronautics—The branch of science that deals with flight and with the operations of all types of aircraft.

Aerostat—A device supported in the air by displacing more than its own weight of air.

AFSS (Automated Flight Service Station)—An air traffic facility that provides pilot briefings and numerous other services.

AGL—Above ground level.

Aircraft—A device that is used or intended to be used for flight in the air.

Airport—An area of land or water that is used for the landing and takeoff of an aircraft.

Altimeter Setting—The station pressure (barometric pressure at the location the reading is taken) which has been corrected for the height of the station above sea level.

Ambient Air—Air surrounding the outside of a balloon envelope.

Anemometer—An instrument used to measure the velocity of moving air.

Apex Line—A line attached to the top of most balloons to assist in inflation or deflation. Also called *crown line* or *top handling line*.

Approved—Approved by the FAA Administrator or person authorized by the Administrator.

Archimedes' Principle—The Greek mathematician's principle of buoyancy, which states that an object (a balloon) immersed in a fluid (the air) loses as much of its own weight as the weight of the fluid it replaces.

ATC—Air Traffic Control.

ATIS (Automatic Terminal Information Service)—The continuous broadcast (by radio or telephone) of recorded noncontrol, essential but routine, information in selected terminal areas.

Aviation—The branch of science, business, or technology that deals with any part of the operation of machines that fly through the air.

AWOS (Automatic Weather Observing System)—Continuous broadcast (by radio or telephone) of weather conditions at selected locations.

Balloon—A lighter-than-air aircraft that is not engine driven, and that sustains flight through the use of either gas buoyancy or an airborne heater.

Balloon Flight Manual—A manual containing operating instructions, limitations, weight, and performance information, that must be available in an aircraft during flight. Portions of the flight manual are FAA-approved.

Basket—Portion of a balloon that carries pilot, passengers, cargo, fuel, and instruments.

Blast—See Burn.

Blast Valve—The valve on a propane burner that controls the flow of propane burned to produce heat.

Bowline Knot—(pronounced boh'-lin) A common knot that is easy to tie and untie and will not slip.

Btu (British thermal unit)—A measurement of heat. The amount of heat required to raise 1 pound of water from 60 to 61 °F.

Buoyancy—In ballooning, when the balloon is zero weight and is neither climbing nor falling.

Burn—A common term meaning to activate the main blast valve and produce a full flame for the purpose of heating the air in the envelope.

Burner—See Heater.

Calendar Month/Year—From a given day or month until midnight of the last day of the month or year.

Capacity—See Volume.

Captive Balloon—Commonly used to describe a balloon that is permanently anchored to the ground.

Category—"(1) As used with respect to the certification, ratings, privileges, and limitations of airmen, means a broad classification of aircraft. Examples include: airplane; rotorcraft glider; and lighter-than-air; and (2) As used with respect to the certification of aircraft, means a grouping of aircraft based upon intended use or operating limitations. Examples include: transport, normal, utility, acrobatic, limited, restricted, and provisional." (14 CFR part 1)

Ceiling—The lowest broken or overcast layer of clouds or vertical visibility into an obscuration.

CFR—Code of Federal Regulations.

Charles' Law—If the pressure of a gas is held constant and its absolute temperature is increased, the volume of the gas will also increase.

Class—"(1) As used with respect to the certification, ratings, privileges, and limitations of airmen, means a classification of aircraft within a category having similar operating characteristics. Examples include: single-engine; multiengine; land; water; gyroplane helicopter; airship; and free balloon; and (2) As used with respect to the certification of aircraft, means a broad grouping of aircraft having similar characteristics of propulsion, flight or landing. Examples include: airplane, rotorcraft, glider, balloon, landplane, and seaplane." (14 CFR part 1)

Coating—A thin synthetic added to the surface of balloon fabric to lessen porosity and ultraviolet-light damage.

Cold Inflation—Forcing cold air into the envelope, giving it some shape to allow heating with the heater.

Commercial Aircraft Operator—"A person who, for compensation or hire, engages in the carriage by aircraft in air commerce of persons or property." (14 CFR part 1)

Commercial Pilot—A person who, for compensation or hire, is certificated to fly an aircraft carrying passengers or cargo.

Controlled Airspace—Airspace designated as Class A, B, C, D, or E within which air traffic control service is provided to some or all aircraft.

Cooling Vent—A vent, in the side or top of the balloon envelope, that opens to release hot air, and that closes after the release of air automatically.

Crew Chief—A crewmember who is assigned the responsibility of organizing and directing other crewmembers.

Crown Line—A line attached to the top of most balloons to assist in the inflation and deflation of the envelope. Sometimes referred to as *apex line* or *top handling line*.

Currency—Common usage for recent flight experience. In order to carry passengers, a pilot must have performed three takeoffs and three landings within the preceding 90 days. In order to carry passengers at night, a pilot must have performed three takeoffs and three landings to a full stop at night (the period beginning 1 hour after sunset and ending 1 hour before sunrise).

Dacron—The registered trade name for polyester fabric developed by DuPont.

Deflation Panel—A panel at the top of the balloon envelope that is deployed at landing to release all hot air (or other lifting gas) from the envelope. A parachute top is a form of deflation panel.

Drag Landing—A high-wind landing where the balloon drags across the ground after the deflation panel has been opened.

Drag Line—A gas balloon term used to describe a large, heavy rope, deployed at landing, which orients the balloon (and rip panel) to the wind, and transfers weight from the balloon to the ground, creating a landing flare.

Drop Line—A rope or webbing, which may be deployed by the pilot to ground crew to assist in landing or ground handling of a balloon.

Envelope—Fabric portion of a balloon that contains hot air or gas.

Equator—The widest diameter of the envelope.

Equilibrium—Equilibrium at launch is typically that temperature at which after the balloon has been inflated and is standing up (erect), the ground crew is able to hold the balloon in place by resting their hands lightly on the basket. When lift equals gravity as in level flight.

FAA (Federal Aviation Administration)—The federal agency responsible to promote aviation safety through regulation and education.

Fabric Test—Testing of the envelope fabric for tensile strength, tear strength, and/or porosity. Fabric tests are specified by each balloon manufacturer.

False Lift—See Uncontrolled Lift.

FCC (Federal Communications Commission)—The federal agency which regulates radio communication and communication equipment in the United States.

Fireproof—Adjective used to describe a noncombustible material that cannot be destroyed by fire.

Flameout—The inadvertent extinguishing of a burner flame.

Flare—The last flight maneuver by an aircraft in a successful landing, wherein the balloon's descent is reduced to a path nearly parallel to the landing surface.

Flexible Suspension—Balloon basket suspension consisting of steel or fiber cables without rigid structure.

Flight Review—Required for all certificated pilots every 24 months in order to retain pilot in command privileges. A flight review consists of at least 1 hour of flight training and 1 hour of ground training.

Flight Time—"The time from the moment the aircraft first moves under its own power for the purpose of flight until the moment it comes to rest at the next point of landing." (14 CFR part 1)

Flight Visibility—"The average forward horizontal distance, of an aircraft in flight, at which prominent unlighted objects may be seen and identified by day and prominent lighted objects may be seen and identified by night." (14 CFR part 1)

FPM—Feet Per Minute.

FSDO (Flight Standards District Office)—Field offices of the FAA, which deal with certification and operation of aircraft.

Gauge—A device for measuring. Required gauges on a hot air balloon are the envelope temperature gauge (pyrometer) and the fuel quantity gauge for each fuel tank. Most balloons also have fuel pressure gauges.

General Aviation—Total field of aviation operations other than military and air transport (airlines).

Gimbal—A type of support that allows a compass or gyroscope to remain in an upright position when its base is tilted.

Gore—A vertical section of fabric, often made of two vertical, or numerous horizontal panels, sewn together to make a balloon envelope.

Grab Test—A test, as specified by balloon manufacturers, to determine the tensile strength of envelope fabric.

Ground Crew—Persons who assist in the assembly, inflation, chase, and recovery of a balloon.

Ground Visibility—"Prevailing horizontal visibility near the earth's surface as reported by the United States National Weather Service or an accredited observer." (14 CFR part 1)

Handling Line—A line, usually 1/4- to 1/2-inch rope, attached to a balloon envelope or basket, used by the pilot or ground crew to assist in the ground handling, inflation, landing, and deflation of a balloon.

Heater—Propane-fueled device to heat air inside the envelope of a balloon, often referred to as a burner.

Helium—A light, inert gaseous chemical element mainly found as a natural gas in the southwestern United States. Used to inflate gas balloons and pilot balloons.

Hydrogen—The lightest of all gaseous elements. Commonly used in Europe for inflating gas balloons. Flammable by itself and explosive when mixed with oxygen. As opposed to helium, hydrogen is easily manufactured.

Hydrostatic Testing—A method of testing propane cylinders wherein the cylinder is filled with water and pressurized.

IFR (Instrument Flight Rules)—Rules governing the procedures for conducting instrument flight. Also a term used by pilots and controllers to indicate type of flight plan.

IFR Conditions—"Weather conditions below the minimums allowed for flight under visual flight rules." (14 CFR part 1)

Igniter—A welding striker, piezo sparker, matches, or other means used to ignite the balloon pilot flame.

Incident—An occurrence other than an accident, associated with the operation of an aircraft, which affects or could affect the safety of operations.

Indicated Altitude—The altitude shown on a properly calibrated altimeter.

Inoperative—Not functioning or not working.

Instructions for Continued Airworthiness—A manual published by an aircraft manufacturer specifying procedures for inspection, maintenance, repair, and mandatory replacement times for life-limited parts.

Instrument—"A device using an internal mechanism to show visually or aurally the attitude, altitude, or operation of an aircraft or aircraft part." (14 CFR part 1) There are only two instruments required in a hot air balloon: vertical speed indicator (VSI) and altimeter.

Jet—The propane metering orifice of a balloon heater where fuel exits to be ignited during a burn.

Life-Limited—An aircraft part whose service is limited to a specified number of operating hours or cycles. For example, some balloon manufacturers require that fuel hoses be replaced after a certain number of years.

Light Aircraft—Any aircraft with a maximum takeoff weight of less than 12,500 pounds. All presently FAA-certificated balloons are light aircraft.

Limitations—Restrictions placed on a balloon by its manufacturer. Examples are maximum envelope temperature and maximum gross weight.

Log—A record of activities: flight, instruction, inspection, and maintenance.

LTA—Lighter-Than-Air.

Maintenance—The upkeep of equipment, to include preservation, repair, overhaul, and the replacement of parts.

Maintenance Manual—A set of detailed instructions issued by the manufacturer of an aircraft, engine, or component that describes the way maintenance should be performed.

Maintenance Release—A release, signed by an authorized inspector, repairman, mechanic or pilot, after work has been performed, stating that an aircraft or aircraft part has been approved for return to service. The person releasing the aircraft must have the authority appropriate to the work being signed off.

Master Tank—The propane tank, usually tank number one, that offers all appropriate services, such as liquid, vapor, and backup system.

Metering Valve—A valve on a balloon heater that can be set to allow propane to pass through at a specific rate.

Methanol—A type of alcohol, usually fermented from wood, required by most balloon manufacturers to be introduced into propane tanks annually to adsorb, and thus eliminate, small quantities of water from the fuel.

Mildew—A gray or white parasite fungus which, under warm, moist conditions, can live on organic dirt found on balloon envelopes. The fungus waste materials attack the coating on the fabric.

Mile—A statute mile is 5,280 feet. A nautical mile is 6,076 feet.

Momentum—The force of a moving body that tries to keep the body moving at the same direction and speed. The momentum weight of the average hot air balloon is nearly 4 tons.

Mooring—Operation of an unmanned balloon secured to the ground by lines or controlled by anything touching the ground. See 14 CFR part 101.

Mouth—The bottom, open end of a hot air balloon envelope. Also called "throat."

Neutral Buoyancy—A condition wherein a balloon is weightless and is neither ascending nor descending.

Next Required Inspection—An annual inspection, or 100-hour inspection, as appropriate.

Night—The time between the end of evening civil twilight and the beginning of morning civil twilight, as published in the American Air Almanac and converted to local time.

Nitrogen Charging—A technique of adding nitrogen gas to propane tanks to increase fuel pressure. Used in place of temperature to control propane pressure in hot air balloons during cold weather.

Non-Destructive Testing—Tests or inspections that when properly performed, will not damage the component or system being tested.

Nonporous—The state of having no pores or openings which will not allow gas to pass through. New hot air balloon fabric is nearly nonporous.

NOTAM (Notice To Airmen)—A notice containing information concerning facilities, services, or procedures, the timely knowledge of which is essential to personnel concerned with flight operations.

Nylon—The registered name for a polymer fabric. Most balloon envelopes are made of nylon.

Operate—"Use, cause to use, or authorize to use aircraft, for the purpose of air navigation including the piloting of aircraft, with or without the right of legal control (as owner, lessee, or otherwise)." (14 CFR part 1)

O-Ring—A doughnut-shaped packing, usually rubber, used between two moving parts to act as a seal. Balloon heater and tank valves usually have O-rings between the valve stem and valve bonnet.

Orographic—A term pertaining to mountains or anything caused by mountains. As in orographic wind—wind formed by mountains. Orographic cloud—a cloud whose existence is caused by disturbed flow of air over and around a mountain barrier.

Overtemp (or Over Temperature)—The act of heating the air inside a hot air balloon envelope beyond the manufacturer's maximum temperature.

Oxygen Starvation—The condition inside a balloon envelope where all available oxygen has been consumed by the heater flame and additional burning is impossible since propane must have oxygen to burn. In extreme cases, the blast flame and pilot light flame will extinguish after a long burn or series of burns and may not relight until the envelope has "breathed" additional air.

Pack—(1) Of balloon envelopes, stuffing the envelope into its storage bag after a flight. (2) Of balloon cold inflation, filling the envelope nearly full of cold air with a very large fan.

Parachute Top—A deflation system wherein the deflation port is sealed with a disc of balloon fabric shaped like a parachute. Lines attached to the edge of the parachute disc gather into a single line that may be pulled down by the pilot in the basket.

Pibal (Pilot Balloon Observations)—A small helium-filled balloon sent aloft to help determine wind direction, velocity, and stability.

PIC (Pilot in Command)—The pilot responsible for the operation and safety of an aircraft during flight.

Piezo—(pronounced pee-ate'zo). A piezoelectric spark generator that is built into many modern balloon heaters to ignite the pilot light.

Pilot Light—A small, continuously burning flame used to ignite the main "blast" flame of a balloon heater.

Pilotage—Navigation by visual reference to landmarks.

Pinhole—Any small hole in a balloon envelope smaller than the maximum dimensions allowed for airworthiness.

Porosity—A condition of the envelope fabric that allows hot air to escape. Excessive porosity requires increased fuel use and results in higher envelope temperatures.

Positive Control—"Control of all air traffic, within designated airspace, by air traffic control." (14 CFR part 1)

Powerplant—The engine or device that propels an airplane, airship, or rotorcraft. The term does not apply to balloons, which are considered to be unpowered aircraft.

Preflight—All preparations, including gathering information, assembly, and inspection performed by the pilot before flight.

Pressure Relief Valve—A device in a propane tank designed to release excess pressure—which may be caused by overfilling, overheating, or excessive nitrogen pressurization—to prevent tank rupture.

Preventive Maintenance—Simple or minor preservation operations and the replacement of small standard parts not involving complex assembly operations.

Prohibited Area—"Designated airspace within which the flight of aircraft is prohibited." (14 CFR part 1)

Propane—A colorless and orderless gas. Ethyl mercaptan is added to propane to give it a detectable odor. Propane weighs 4.2 lbs. per gallon.

PTS (Practical Test Standard)—Book containing areas of knowledge and skill that a person must demonstrate competency in for the issuance of pilot certificates or ratings.

Pull Test—A strength test in which a section of envelope fabric is pulled to a definite pound measurement to determine if it meets the certification requirements for airworthiness.

Pyrometer—An instrument used to measure air temperature inside the top of a balloon envelope.

Rapid Descent—A relatively fast loss of altitude. A subjective term, but usually meant to describe a descent of more than 500 FPM.

Rating—"A statement that, as part of a pilot certificate, sets forth special conditions, privileges, or limitations." (14 CFR part 1)

Red Line—Refers to a line which activates the deflation panel of a balloon, or the maximum envelope temperature allowed, or the maximum on a gauge.

Repair Station—A facility where specified aircraft and their parts may be inspected, repaired, altered, modified, or maintained. FAA approval is issued to a facility upon qualifications specified by the local FSDO.

Repairman Certificate—An FAA certificate issued to a person who is employed by a repair station or air carrier as a specialist in some form of aircraft maintenance. A repairman certificate is also issued to an eligible person who is the primary builder of an experimental aircraft, to which the privileges of the certificate are applicable.

Required Equipment—Equipment that must be aboard an aircraft, as required either by the FAA or balloon manufacturer, to maintain airworthiness.

Restricted Area—Airspace of defined dimensions within which the flight of aircraft is restricted in accordance with certain conditions.

Return to Service—A certificated mechanic or authorized inspector must approve an aircraft for return to service after it has been inspected, repaired, or altered. In addition, an aircraft that has been modified must be test flown by an appropriately certificated pilot before return to service.

Rip Panel—A deflation panel, usually circular or triangular, at the top of a balloon envelope, which may be opened by pulling a line in the basket to allow hot air or gas to escape, and the envelope to deflate.

Rotator Vent—See Turning Vent.

SIGMET—Significant Meteorological Information.

Small Aircraft—Aircraft having a maximum certificated takeoff weight of 12,500 pounds or less. All currently type-certificated balloons are small aircraft.

S/N (Serial Number)—A number, usually one of a series, assigned for identification.

Step Descent—A method of allowing a balloon to lower toward the ground by reducing the altitude, leveling-off, and repeating the step, to lower the balloon in increments rather than one continuous motion.

Superheat—A gas balloon term, superheat occurs when the sun heats the gas inside the envelope to a temperature exceeding that of the ambient air, resulting in expansion of the gas.

Superpressure Balloon—(1) A type of hot air balloon which has no openings to the atmosphere—the mouth is sealed with a special skirt—and is kept pumped full of air (at a higher pressure than the atmosphere) by an on-board fan. Used on moored balloons to allow operations in relatively strong wind. (2) In gas ballooning a sealed envelope in which the internal envelope pressure exceeds that of a non-sealed envelope.

Suspension Lines—Lines descending from the mouth of a balloon envelope from which the basket and heater are suspended.

Temperature Gauge—The thermometer system, required in all type-certificated hot air balloons, that gives a constant reading of the inside air temperature at the top of the envelope. May be direct reading, or remote, using a thermocouple or thermistor connected to a gauge in the basket or reading signals sent by a transmitter.

Temperature Recorder—A small plastic laminate with temperature-sensitive paint dots that turn from white or silver to black, to record permanently the maximum temperature reached.

Tensile Strength—The strength of a material that resists the stresses of trying to stretch or lengthen it.

Terminal Velocity Descent—A term used by balloonists for the speed obtained when the balloon is allowed to fall until it apparently stops accelerating, at which point the envelope acts as a parachute and its vertical speed is no longer affected by its lifting gas, but only by its shape (which is caused by design), load, and other factors.

Tethering—Operation of a manned balloon secured to the ground by a series of lines.

Tetrahedron—A large triangular-shaped wind indicator mounted on a pivot so it can swing free and point into the wind. Usually found at airports.

Thermal—A column of rising air associated with adjacent areas of differing temperature. Thermal activity caused by the sun's heating usually starts 2 to 3 hours after sunrise.

Throttle Valve—See Blast Valve.

Time in Service—"With respect to maintenance time records, means the time from the moment an aircraft leaves the surface of the earth until it touches it at the next point of landing." (14 CFR part 1)

Touch-and-Go Landing—An operation by an aircraft that lands and takes off without stopping.

Traffic Pattern—The traffic flow that is prescribed for aircraft landing at or taking off from an airport.

Turning Vent—A vent on the side of a hot air balloon envelope which, when opened, allows escaping air to exit in a manner causing the balloon to rotate on its axis.

Type Certification—Official recognition that the design and operating limitations of an aircraft, engine, or propeller meet the airworthiness standards prescribed by the Code of Federal Regulations for that particular category or type of aircraft, engine, or propeller.

Uncontrolled Lift—Lift that occurs without specific action by the pilot. Often referred to as false lift.

Variometer—See VSI (Vertical Speed Indicator).

Vent—Verb: "to vent" is the action of opening the vent to cool the air in the envelope. Noun: an envelope opening that will automatically close.

Vent Line—The line that activates the cooling vent.

VFR (Visual Flight Rules)—Flight rules governing aircraft flight when the pilot has visual reference to the ground at all times.

VHF (Very High Frequency)—The frequency range used for air/ground voice and navigational facility communications.

Virga—Precipitation that falls from a cloud and evaporates before reaching the ground.

Volume—The total amount of air or gas (expressed in cubic feet) contained in a balloon envelope.

VSI (Vertical Speed Indicator)—An instrument that continuously records the rate at which an aircraft climbs or descends. Usually measured in FPM. A required instrument in a balloon.

Warp—The threads in a piece of fabric that run the length of the fabric.

Weigh-Off—Determine neutral buoyancy of a gas balloon or airship by taking weight off at launch.

Wind Direction—Wind direction is always expressed by the direction the wind is coming from.

Wind Shear—A strong and sudden shift in wind speed or direction, which may be either vertical or horizontal. Wind shear should not be confused with normal wind change, which is gentler. Wind shear is often associated with the passage of a weather front, or a strong temperature inversion.

Wind Sock—A long, tapered cloth tube, open at both ends, mounted on an elevated pole, and allowed to pivot. The large end is supported and held open by a circular ring and points toward the wind.

ISBN 0-16-050838-X
90000
9 780160 508387